MECHANICS' INSTITUTE
MECHANICS'
MERCANTILE LIBRARY

Marketing Your Consulting and Professional Services

Other Books by Richard A. Connor, Jr.

Getting New Clients, with Jeffrey P. Davidson
Increasing Revenue from Your Clients

Other Books by Jeffrey P. Davidson

Selling to the Giants: How to Become a Key Supplier to Large Corporations
Marketing for the Home-Based Business
The Marketing Sourcebook for Small Business
Marketing on a Shoestring
Avoiding the Pitfalls of Starting Your Own Business
Getting New Clients, with Richard A. Connor, Jr.
Blow Your Own Horn
Power and Protocol
The Achievement Challenge: How to Be a "10" in Business, with Don Beveridge
How to Have a Great Year Every Year, with Dave Yoho

SECOND EDITION

Marketing Your Consulting and Professional Services

DICK CONNOR, CMC   **JEFFREY P. DAVIDSON, CMC**

John Wiley & Sons, Inc.

New York • Chichester • Brisbane • Toronto • Singapore

Library of Congress Cataloging in Publication Data

Connor, Dick
    Marketing your consulting and professional services / Dick
Connor, Jeffrey P. Davidson. — 2nd ed.
        p.   cm.
    Includes bibliographical references.
    ISBN 0-471-52074-8
        1. Professions—Marketing—Handbooks, manuals, etc.
    2. Consultants—Marketing—Handbooks, manuals, etc.   I. Davidson,
Jeffrey P.   II. Title.
    HD69.C6C63   1990
658.8—dc20   90-12198
                                                        CIP

Printed in the United States of America

10   9   8   7   6   5   4   3   2

This book is dedicated to
Emanuel Davidson
who knew full well
of its creation
years before its authors

and to
Susan Connor
for her support
during our
formative years

Preface

This book is designed to be *used* by every service provider who wants to survive and thrive in the 1990s and beyond. We believe that continued profitable growth is best accomplished by promoting and providing solutions to important needs faced by your most desirable current clients and high-potential prospective clients in targeted industry-market niches.

The niche approach enables the busy service provider to *leverage* his or her time, talents, and experience to sense, sell, serve, and satisfy the needs of targeted clients and prospects in a niche. It allows you to work from your comfort zone, that area of professional behavior where you are confident, productive, and effective. Working from your comfort zone also means calling on those clients, prospects, and suspects with whom you already have some familiarity and affinity.

We have written this second edition to be a marketing handbook for the 1990s and beyond. It contains principle-based practices and strategies forged by over 35 years' experience in the trenches serving more than 600 firms worldwide, and converting normative theory into practical reality. It is for busy professionals who want to know what to do and how.

This edition dramatically extends and broadens the client-centered marketing approach we introduced in 1985. The approach has now evolved into a practical "deliverables-driven" marketing *system* for penetrating a targeted niche. You can now analyze your existing practice to determine much more precisely the targets of opportunity and targets of attention that deserve the application of client-centered marketing principles and techniques.

Every chapter has been updated to be relevant to the marketing situations you will face in the 1990s. Nine new chapters have been added. As with the first edition, the emphasis is on developing a plan for action. The inclusion of a revised personal marketing plan, which is now keyed to the various chapters, is a further valuable enhancement.

Marketing Your Consulting and Professional Services is a how-to-do-it book for the busy professional now in practice or planning to go into practice. Written both for the individual who is a solo consultant and the one who is a member of a firm, the focus is on marketing effectiveness: doing the right things, and doing them on a timely basis.

Our goal is to help you understand the core concepts and principles, and then to show you how to make them a reality in your own practice. This revised edition is designed to be an action guide for readers from a broad range of experience. It is excellent for the beginner because no prior knowledge of services marketing is needed; everything is explained in a logical step-by-step approach. For readers who have had some experience in services marketing, this book will fill in any gaps and make it easier to explore and use some of the more sophisticated principles you may have not yet employed in your practice. And even for the "seasoned pro," the book provides a manual to use in training others in a logical manner.

Dick Connor, CMC   Jeffrey P. Davidson, CMC
Springfield, Virginia   *Falls Church, Virginia*

Acknowledgments

The authors wish to acknowledge Maggie Bedrosian, Robert Bookman, Nelson Cover, Richard Cupka, Bruce Harrison, Ted Eisenberg, Karen Kalish, Chester Karrass, Ph.D., E. Jerome McCarthy, Ph.D., and James McClain for their subject matter expertise. Also thanks to Andrea Yurich for reviewing the galleys, Willis Shen for preparing the index, Judy Dubler for word processing, Laura Cleveland and WordCrafters for copy editing and production, and Karl Weber for overseeing the completion of this second edition.

Contents

APPENDICES

List of Figures

PART ONE

Foundations

Professional service firms, once virtually immune to and protected from "distasteful" practices such as promotion and personal selling, must now operate in an environment that is characterized by rampant commercialism and impacted by rapid and radical changes.

We have found that the most successful professional service firms across a vast array of industries have geared their practice toward the needs of the client and primary market, as opposed to offering those services that the professional happens to be good at or can readily provide. We have termed this approach to marketing professional and consulting services *client-centered marketing*.

Client-centered marketing necessitates continual relationship development. All the professional's experience, planning, and action are targeted toward the needs of the client.

A *client-centered orientation* reduces the need for individual professionals to acquire and employ sophisticated and aggressive personal selling skills and expensive sales supports. The professional's goal is to sit mentally on the client's side of the desk to view the client's operations and needs through objective eyes. Thus the professional is able to identify ways to assist the client in doing better what the client is in business to do. This is really an advocate-oriented relationship.

Part One introduces the client-centered marketing approach, the notions of leveraging your time, talents, and technology and working within your personal marketing comfort zone. The client-centered marketing system is explained and sets the stage for subsequent chapters.

CHAPTER 1

The Client-Centered Marketing Approach

This chapter introduces the client-centered marketing system. We believe it is the *only* marketing system that will enable you to survive and prosper in the 1990s and beyond. After reading this chapter and absorbing the ideas, you will be able to:

☐ Define client-centered marketing for yourself and enlist others in participating and in creating such a program.

☐ Explain to others how client-centered marketing differs from traditional and hard-sell marketing approaches and why you have adopted a client-centered approach for your practice.

☐ Identify marketing objectives that need to be and can be achieved through your client-centered marketing program.

☐ Define leveraging in your own terms and appreciate the potential impact it has in your practice.

☐ Relate the notion of marketing comfort zones to your situation.

☐ Answer the question: "If clients don't purchase services, what *do* they purchase from me?"

Client-centered marketing is the development of a special type of client-firm relationship with your most desirable clients, prospective clients, and referral relationships within targeted niches. Once the special relationship is established, the primary and continuing task is to *sense, sell, serve,* and *satisfy* the needs and expectations of these clients and others in ways that are mutually profitable.

A WORKING DEFINITION

Client-centered marketing is the strategic decision to

1. Select a targeted industry-market niche(s) for special attention.
2. Develop and enhance relationships with high-potential clients, prospective clients, and niche influentials.
3. Prepare, position, promote, and provide value-perceived solutions for selected needs of targeted clients and prospective clients in the niche.
4. Leverage the time, technology, and resources available to you as you serve in ways that result in mutual satisfaction and retention of the client-firm relationship.

SOME OTHER ESSENTIAL DEFINITIONS

Choosing an industry-market niche for concentration is one of the most important strategic decisions you make regarding the long-term viability of your practice. You can't be all things to all people, and you certainly can't be all things to all clients. To survive and thrive in today's business environment you must direct your attention to niches that you can penetrate and where you can most readily serve prosperously.

The term *industry* here refers to a specific four-digit Standard Industry Code (SIC) classification as defined by the U.S. Department of Commerce. *Market* is synonymous with the postal ZIP codes that comprise your practice area for a specific SIC. *Niche* is used as an abbreviation for industry-market niche and includes clients, prospective clients, suspects, nonclient influentials, competitors, and others who serve and interact with the niche in some way.

Not for Every Client

A client-centered marketing and client service approach is not appropriate for all clients. Rather, it is reserved for the 20 percent of your existing clients and targeted prospects that predictably may represent 80 percent of your current opportunities. The goal of client-centered marketing is to increase the number of high-potential clients and prospective clients representing opportunity.

The remaining 80 percent of your current clients and prospects are served in a business-as-usual manner. Since you are a *busy* professional who struggles daily with finding and allocating time for new business development, we stress the principle of leveraging your time, talents, and technology.

MARKETING OBJECTIVES

Eight major marketing objectives can be accomplished through a client-centered marketing program:

1. Generating controlled, profitable growth
2. Expanding services to existing clients
3. Retaining desirable clients
4. Upgrading or replacing undesirable clients
5. Capitalizing on the potential within your existing practice
6. Managing your image with clients and targets
7. Attracting desirable prospective clients
8. Transforming your current practice into a desired/required future practice

Each of these objectives is covered in detail in later chapters.

CLIENT-CENTERED MARKETING VERSUS OTHER APPROACHES

To understand why a client-centered marketing approach is stressed, it is helpful to contrast it with two other major approaches to marketing available to the professional—the traditional and the hard sell.

The *traditional* approach is basically a reactive one. The underlying assumption is that growth is solely the result of providing good technical services and meeting the existing demands of the marketplace. Thus encouragement of growth involves very little strategy or coordination of effort.

It's been said that, "Doing what you've always done will get you what you've always gotten." Adherence to the traditional marketing orientation—waiting for the client to contact the professional on recognition of a need or problem—will seldom produce the additional new business required in today's intensely competitive situation. Too often a second, more aggressive firm is working to be next in line if you fail to anticipate needs.

Existing client problems are dealt with as they arise and are brought to the attention of the professional. Often, it is too late or too expensive to correct these problems and the disappointed client is inclined to replace the firm or cut back on the amount of additional work authorized. Usually, no organized prospecting programs for attracting eligible potential clients have been developed since referrals are taken for granted as the result of "doing a good job." In today's competitive market, these assumptions can be very costly.

The other approach is known as the *hard sell*. Those following the hard-sell approach focus on getting out and getting known in their practice areas. Instead of focusing on client needs, they place the emphasis on "our firm," "our services," and "our reputation," assuming that growth is largely the result of being known in the community. This approach can be successful in the short run, since it will attract some price-sensitive clients looking for a good deal.

The hard-sell approach has two major drawbacks. Some of the new business is questionable in terms of real and lasting value since these same clients may shop elsewhere later and also because quality clients eventually tire of an approach that is not sensitive to their needs.

An audit services firm instituted a hard-sell approach that involved contacting influentials such as lending officers, prominent attorneys, and others and soliciting referrals from them. Monthly goals were set for each of the partners and managers by the partner in charge. After several months the program died an obscure death. Several years later the partner in charge was still wondering why his troops didn't see the light.

LEVERAGING

The notion of leveraging is integral to effective client-centered marketing. The dictionary defines leverage as "the advantage or gained power from an action." In marketing terms, leveraging is the process of identifying and capitalizing on the *smallest* number of actions that produce the *greatest* results.

Leveraging your time and the time of your staff and other scarce and costly resources is essential. Your firm's primary task is to sense, serve, and satisfy the needs of its clients at a reasonable profit while handling an increasingly expanding "pending actions" list. You need to make certain that every minute devoted to marketing counts.

MARKETING COMFORT ZONE

Frequently when speaking to clients and other groups, Dick mentions that he is a scuba diver. His current comfort zone is in the 50- to 60-foot range. Diving at this depth, he is alert and relaxed, enjoying himself and not preoccupied with surviving the dive.

He then relates diving to your current *marketing* comfort zone, and defines this as the current range of effective self-initiated behavior where you are productive, confident, and forthright in communications and actions. The knowledge, skills, and attitudes you have acquired by serving your best clients in the niche constitute a large portion of your current marketing comfort zone.

The value in using the client-centered marketing approach is that you work primarily in the current comfort zone. This is in direct contrast to a hard-sell approach, which often involves making cold selling calls and trying to pitch your services to disinterested people who wish you would go away.

MARKETING IN PERSPECTIVE

Our experience in working with or speaking before professional service firms in many segments indicates that without major program status, marketing is seldom effective and long-lasting.

A successful professional practice can be compared with a balanced four-legged stool:

Leg 1 is technical quality: consistent, superb service delivered on a timely basis.

Leg 2 is personnel: selecting, training, developing, motivating, and retaining the best staff available.

Leg 3 is financial administration.

Leg 4 is client-centered marketing: sensing, selling, serving, and satisfying the needs of present and potential clients to provide the best services available.

Client-centered marketing is essentially relationship development, and the relationship is based on a complex array of technical and personal factors that create a high degree of interdependence. The client is the target and the beneficiary of all the professional's experience, planning, and actions.

Professionals who are effective in marketing have learned along the way to develop relationships with those clients and others who are readily willing and able to assist them in their various marketing and selling activities. They search constantly for the relatively few key contacts who facilitate leveraging of resources, to achieve results with the minimum expenditure of time and energy. In short, you must recognize the fact that not all clients are created equally.

Effective client-centered marketing requires acknowledgement that:

1. Clients don't purchase services, but rather purchase your promise to produce a more favorable future for them on schedule, within budget, and in a manner that meets their expectations. One exceptionally able professional made it a practice to surface the client's expectations regarding the final product or "deliverable" by asking the question: "How will you and I know when I'm doing the job you expect me to do?" The answer to this question invariably surfaces both reasonable and unrealistic expectations that need to be negotiated.

2. Services are really bought or rejected in the "gut" by clients, and the decision is justified to themselves and others by the use of hard copy such as proposals and testimonials.

3. Value is always defined by the recipient, not the provider. It is always rooted in needs systems. Value is a function of needs being identified and satisfied in ways that meet expectations.

Having introduced client-centered marketing, we turn to a detailed discussion of the client-centered marketing system.

CHAPTER 2

The Client-Centered Marketing System

Four elements make up the client-centered marketing system, and each is described in this chapter. Careful examination of the four elements will enable you to:

☐ Apply the principle of leveraging to your client marketing and service efforts.

☐ Work within your current comfort zone.

☐ Determine the strategic implications of your existing practice and marketing approaches or techniques.

☐ Employ service marketing terms with confidence and precision as you explain your new ideas to others in your firm.

ELEMENTS OF THE MARKETING SYSTEM

The four major elements include the following:

- Existing practice factors
- Existing referral sources
- Targets of opportunity, attention, and influence
- Strategic new business development factors

Figure 2–1 shows the contents and flow of each of these four elements and their relationship to each other. Each element can be managed separately and in conjunction with one or more of the other elements.

The existing practice factors element is comprised of five distinct variables:

1. *Your existing clients* and the potential opportunity, growth, and problems they represent. Your existing clients can be broadly classified as "desirable," "unknown potential at this time," and "undesirable."

2. *Prospective clients* in your "pending new business file." A prospective client is a nonclient with whom you have had a business discussion and proposed a service solution. You are now waiting for approval to proceed with the engagement.

3. *Recent and planned financial performance* is expressed in terms of fee volume, net profit, billable hours, managed hours, and known or suspected revenue surplus/gap for the next planning period.

FIGURE 2–1
The Client-Centered Marketing System

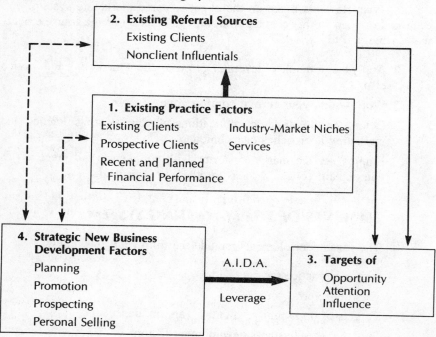

4. *Existing industry-market niches served* and the potential they represent for growth and competition is the fourth item comprising the existing practice factor.

In Chapter 1 we defined *industry* as an SIC grouping, a group of similar organizations and individuals that address the same general needs of their clients and customers through the delivery of their goods and services.

Your *markets* are the geographic arenas—ZIP codes—in which you promote and conduct your practice, or in the case of international markets the countries or geographic areas.

A *niche* is a targeted SIC–ZIP combination.

5. *Your existing services* represent the percent of total fees generated by each, their degree of client-centeredness, and the nature of their technology—state-of-the-art, competitive, or lagging.

The second element in the system is *existing referral sources*. The two classes of referrals are as follows:

1. *Existing key client executives and individuals* whom you serve who are especially satisfied with the way they are served and provide you with leads, give you written testimonials, and involve you in their professional and trade association activities.

2. *Nonclient influentials* includes attorneys, bankers, editors, executive directors of industry associations, community leaders, and others who provide you with leads, favorably influence your desirable prospective clients regarding your ability to deliver on your promises, or serve your clients in noncompetitive ways.

Of the four major elements in the client-centered marketing system, the two just discussed—existing practice factors and existing referral relationships—form the bedrock of your current practice. It is here that you live and work and generate your current and short-term billable hours.

Both elements exist within your current marketing comfort zone, the area in which you are able to comfortably and confidently initiate and respond to new business discussions with existing clients who need and want your services.

The third element, targets, includes the lesser, concentrated number of clients, prospects, suspects, niches, and services for which you leverage your time, and is comprised of three categories:

1. *Targets of opportunity* include existing desirable clients with unmet needs, prospective clients in your new business pipeline, desirable potential clients, and targeted industry-market niches.

2. *Targets of attention* include all existing practice factors that warrant your focused attention in the next marketing period—month, quarter, or year.

3. *Targets of influence* refer to additional nonclient influentials whom you seek to develop as referral sources. These targets of influence include attorneys, executive directors of trade associations, and so on.

The fourth element, strategic new business development factors, includes four interrelated activities:

1. *Planning* refers to the strategic plans that guide the future development of the firm, annual marketing plans that allocate the resources to be applied to opportunities and problems, periodic campaign-specific planning, and individual planning that converts the broad goals into specific objectives and action steps.

2. *Promotion* refers to the activities involved in managing your business image and reputation to maximize the impact on your targets of opportunity, attention, and influence.

3. *Prospecting* is the process of identifying high-potential "suspect" individuals and organizations in your industry-market niches, and then contacting decision makers within those organizations to obtain an appointment with them to discuss a known or suspected need that you are equipped to handle. Once a decision maker in a targeted firm, or an individual, agrees to meet with you, that person becomes a "prospect."

4. *Personal selling* refers to the face-to-face new business discussions you plan for and conduct with clients, prospective clients, and suspects in your practice area.

This chapter has presented an overview of the client-centered marketing system, which will be more fully described in subsequent chapters. In the next chapter we discuss an essential information gathering and analysis task that, when completed, enables you to analyze your existing practice factors and set your targets of opportunity, attention, and influence.

PART TWO

The Action Inventory

Part Two is the get-ready step. In this pivotal section you are shown how to take an action inventory of your existing practice factors (Element 1 in the client-centered marketing system) and your existing referral sources (Element 2 in the marketing system).

You will see how to prepare a data input work sheet from which four practice profiles can be prepared, a current prospects profile, and two profiles showing your current referral sources. The results of this analysis prepare you for Part Three, in which your targets of opportunity, targets of attention, and targets of influence are identified. The diagram on the next page shows how these targets will be developed.

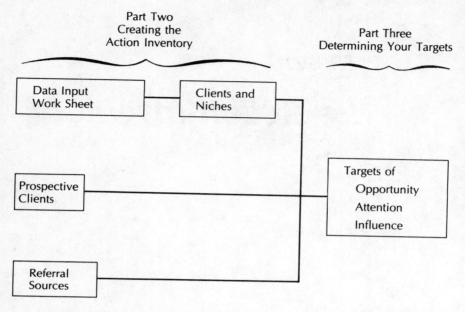

The procedures in this part and the next will show you step-by-step how to build your marketing information system.

CHAPTER 3

Getting Started by Taking Stock

This chapter focuses on creating a system for acquiring and analyzing essential marketing information, a core component of a client-centered marketing system. After reading this chapter and performing the computations, you will be able to:

☐ Identify essential information for assembly in developing your marketing program.

☐ Prepare a data input work sheet.

☐ Perform a macrolevel analysis of your processed information in preparation for the chapters that follow.

A WORD OF ADVICE

The marketing information system presented in this book will serve you as long as you are in practice, and completing this chapter will start you on your way. Please don't shortcut the recommended steps. Assembling and processing the information is a significant task that yields a measure of control over your practice and enables you to effectively leverage your time, talents, and technology.

The data input worksheet in Figure 3–1 will assist you in compiling the information needed to analyze your practice factors. A spreadsheet program can be used to enter and compute the information. A template program is available from the senior author.

Each column on the work sheet will be discussed in terms of the data required, the calculations, and the use of the processed information.

ORGANIZE YOUR INFORMATION

1. Rank your current clients in descending order of revenues obtained from them during the most recent 12 months. If you serve several clients in the same industry belonging to a parent company whom you also serve, group all of these clients and consider them as one. Your goal is to determine the current and potential level of penetration in each industry-market niche you now serve.

2. Assemble your prospective clients in the pipeline information—remember, a prospective client is a nonclient with whom you have had a new business discussion, but whom you have not yet converted into a new client.

3. Assemble your accounts receivable information.

4. Refer to your work in process records.

5. Reflect on the amount of unexpected or planned-on revenue that historically has come to you "over-the-transom" in recent years.

6. Prepare Figure 3–1, "Data Input Work Sheet."

7. Prepare your spreadsheet program to compute and present the results of columns 2, 3, and 4 as shown in Figure 3–1.

   • Column 2 contains all the revenue received from clients served and billed during the previous 12 months.

   • Column 3 contains your estimate of fees to be generated during the next 12 months from each revenue source.

   • Column 4 presents the percentage of total fees represented by each revenue source.

ENTER YOUR INFORMATION

1. List the names of clients from whom fees were received during the previous 12 months in Column 1 in descending order of fees received.

2. Enter the total fees received during the 12-month period in Column 2 for each client listed in Column 1.

3. For each client listed in Column 1 whom you will continue to serve during the next 12 months, estimate the anticipated fees you will collect during this period and enter this amount in Column 3.

4. For each client served and billed during the most recent 12-month period that you will not serve during the next period, enter the fee amount shown in Column 2 as a dollar amount in Column 3.

5. Now list in Column 1 the names of clients you are now serving for the first time and will bill during the next 12 months. Enter the estimated fees in Column 3.

6. In Column 1 list the names of recently added clients you will serve for the first time later in this period. Enter the estimated fees in Column 3.

7. Enter the name of current prospective clients in Column 1. Enter the estimated amount to be billed and received from the conversion of these prospective clients into new clients in Column 3 as + amounts.

8. Enter the amount expected from collecting on your accounts receivable during the next period in Column 3.

9. Enter the amount expected to be received from currently listed work in process records in Column 3.

10. Finally, enter the amount of unexpected or planned-on new revenue you expect to come to you "over-the-transom" and enter this in Column 3.

You now have the basis for a realistic targeted revenue budget for the next 12 months. The dollar difference between the total estimated revenue shown in Column 3 and the revenue goals for the coming period provides you with the level of additional new business effort required to achieve the revenue goal for the coming period.

11. In Column 5, enter the four-digit SIC code for each client and prospective client listed in Column 1. Refer to Appendix A for a list of the codes for each industry.

Leave Columns 6 and 7 blank for now. You will use the completed work sheet in the next chapter when you classify each client and prospective client as either a target of opportunity or a target of attention.

PROCESSING YOUR DATA

1. Compute the total fees received as shown in Column 2.

2. Compute the total estimated fees to be received during the next 12 months and show this in Column 3.

Figure 3–1
Data Input Work Sheet

1	2	3
Revenue Sources	*Previous 12 Months' Fees*	*Estimated Next 12 Months' Fees*
Clients served and billed in previous 12 months		
Clients being served for first time and not yet billed		
Clients to be served later this period		
Prospects to be converted this period		
Accounts Receivable Work in Process Other		
Totals		

3. Compute the percentage of total fees for each client and prospective client as shown in Column 4.

4. Compute the total estimated fees and percentage of fees for each SIC code, and array them from largest to smallest.

With this one calculation you can now identify your current primary and secondary industry concentrations. A primary industry has a relatively

4	5	6	7
% of Total Estimated Fees	*Niche SIC Number*	*Client Class*	*Target Class*
100%			

large percentage of total fees. A secondary industry has a relatively small percentage of total fees. You will use this information in Chapter 7.

You now have the basic inputs for undertaking a marketing-centered analysis of your current practice elements. With these steps behind you, you are now ready to proceed to Chapter 4, where you will classify your current clients.

CHAPTER 4

Classifying Your Current Clients

This chapter focuses on the activities involved in classifying and assessing the potential of your existing clients. On completion, you will be able to answer the following questions:

☐ How do "A," "B," "C," "D," and "U" clients differ?

☐ Why must "A," "B," "C," "D," and "U" clients be treated differently?

☐ Why is it harmful to give "C" and "D" clients "A" level of attention?

☐ Which clients represent targets of opportunity or targets of attention?

ALL CLIENTS ARE NOT EQUAL

Classifying your present clients is a major step toward capitalizing on areas of opportunity within your practice. Your primary purpose is to identify opportunities for leveraging your existing client base.

Leveraging your existing client base requires that you:

1. Classify your existing clients using our suggested "A," "B," "C," "D," and "U" approach.

2. Determine your current targets of opportunity and targets of attention.

CLASSIFICATION 101

Begin by referring to Figure 3–1. You are now ready to complete Column 6, "Client Class." Use Figure 4–1, which summarizes the characteristics of "A," "B," "C," "D," and "U" clients, to classify each client served during the previous 12 months and for whom you have listed estimated fees to be generated during the next 12 months, and place the proper letter designation for each in Column 6. The new clients to be served for the first time during this period should be assigned a "U" classification.

LEVERAGE THE "A"s

Your "A" clients should account for a substantial portion of your revenue and provide you with growth opportunities. Remember, an "A" is an extremely desirable client. This type of client provides you with substantial

FIGURE 4–1
Criteria for Classifying Your Existing Clients

Desirable Clients

1. "A" Clients: Clients that make referrals to others in your behalf have strong potential for fee growth, are receptive to additional constructive service ideas, and frequently provide you with excellent opportunities to develop your skills and information base. Also include here "B" clients you hope will develop into "A" clients. They willingly pay their fees, are generally receptive to additional service discussions, and may be educated into making referrals at a later date.

2. "B" Clients: These clients are your bread and butter clients. They pay their bills, don't give you too much grief, but do not represent potential for good fee growth.

Unknown at This Time—"U" Clients

1. Clients whom you are now serving for the first time
2. Newly acquired clients whom you are yet to begin serving
3. Other existing clients not yet classified

Undesirable Clients

1. "C" Clients: These clients seek discounts and additional free services, and are frequently slow in paying invoices.

2. "D" Clients: These are the clients you wish you had never accepted in the first place. They often operate on the margin of ethical performance and are not adverse to pressuring you to compromise your personal and professional standards.

3. "X" Clients: "A" clients with warning signals.

FIGURE 4–2
Existing "A" Clients

1	2	3	4
		Potential for Additional Services	
Client	Referral Resources?	Short-Term* H,M,L†	Long-Term** H,M,L†

*12 months
**beyond 12 months
†H = high potential; M = medium potential; L = low potential
††1 = poor; 4 = perfect

5	6	7
Quality of Relationship 1–4[††]	Target Classification	Next Steps

revenue, may make referrals in your behalf, provides you with potential for additional services, and so forth. Develop the habit of capturing additional information about them. Figure 4–2 is a convenient form for this purpose.

Remember, all of this analysis is designed to simplify your marketing task by pointing out the clients you should be serving in client-centered ways.

To complete Figure 4–2:

1. List the names of your "A" clients in descending fee order in Column 1.

2. If a client is a referral source, write "Yes" in Column 2.

3. Enter the potential for providing additional services in the next 12 months in Column 3. Write "H" for high potential, "M" for medium potential, or "L" for low potential.

4. Enter the potential for providing additional services beyond the next 12 months in Column 4. Write "H" for high potential, "M" for medium potential, or "L" for low potential.

5. Assess the current quality of relationship with each client. Using a scale of 1, which is a poor relationship, up to 4, which is a perfect relationship, assign the proper number for each client in Column 5. Any relationship that is assessed a 2 or 1 automatically becomes a target of attention with the letter "A" listed in Column 6.

6. Assign the appropriate target classification letter for each client: "O" for opportunity, "A" for attention.

Figure 4–3 summarizes the characteristics of targets of opportunity and targets of attention. Refer to this figure to make the proper classification in Column 6 on Figure 4–2. Note that not every client will receive a target classification. Remember, the goal is to enable you to leverage your time by identifying which clients require your special attention at this time.

Complete Figure 4–2 by listing in Column 7 the steps you need to take next, given your assessment. For example, to improve the primary client-firm relationship, or to pre-sell a needed additional service.

UPGRADE THE "B"s

Use the chart in Figure 4–4 to list any "B" clients that have new business potential or could be upgraded to "A" clients with a reasonable investment of time on your part.

To complete Figure 4–4:

1. List the names of your "B" clients with potential for additional services or upgrading in descending fee order in Column 1.

FIGURE 4–3
Current Target Categories

Targets of Opportunity

1. Existing "A" and "B" clients with needs for additional services who possess a budget for your services and are willing to discuss their needs with you
2. Existing prospective clients

Targets of Attention

1. "B" clients with potential for upgrading to "A"
2. "Unknown" clients who need to be classified
3. Undesirable "C" clients who can be upgraded by reducing discounts or speeding up payment of invoices
4. Other potential clients in your geographic area needing to be contacted
5. "A" clients with warning signals:
    - Known/suspected to be dissatisfied with your services
    - Targeted by other firms
    - Key clients no longer making referrals
    - No longer receptive to discussing additional services
    - Engagements are no longer profitable
    - May be merger candidates
    - Quality of relationship is 1 or 2
6. Undesirable clients with warning signals:
    - "C" clients for whom discounts or receivables are growing
    - "D" clients who are becoming more troublesome or risky to retain

---

2. If a client is a referral source, write "Yes" in Column 2.

3. Next, enter the potential for providing additional services in the next 12 months in Column 3. Write "H" for high potential, "M" for medium potential, or "L" for low potential.

4. Enter the potential for providing additional services beyond the next 12 months in Column 4. Write "H" for high potential, "M" for medium potential, or "L" for low potential.

5. Assess the current quality of relationship with each client. Using a scale of 1, which is a poor relationship, up to 4, which is a perfect relationship, assign the proper number for each client in Column 5.

FIGURE 4–4
Existing "B" Clients

1	2	3	4
		Potential for Additional Services	
Client	Referral Resources?	Short-Term* H,M,L†	Long-Term** H,M,L†

*12 months
**beyond 12 months
†H = high potential; M = medium potential; L = low potential
‡1 = poor; 4 = perfect

5	6	7
Quality of Relationship 1–4[‡]	Target Classification	Next Steps

Figure 4–5
Existing "C" and "D" Clients

1	2		3	
	a.	b.	a. Previous 12 Months' Fees	b. Percentage of Total Fees
Client	"C"	"D"		
Totals			100%	

"C" = excessive discount or collection problems
"D" = a problem client that makes you vulnerable

Any relationship assessed a 2 or 1 automatically becomes a target of attention, "A."

CORRECT THE CAUSES OF "C"s

Your "C" clients make their presence known quickly as they haggle over fees, want scope changes without paying you for extra time, and give you the "check is in the mail" routine when their past due receivables are brought to their attention.

	4	5
c. *Estimated* *Next 12 Months'* *Fees*	*Target* *of* *Attention?*	*Next Steps*

Use Figure 4–5 to list your current undesirable "C" and "D" clients.

1. List the names of undesirable clients in Column 1.
2. Place a check in Column 2a if the client is a fee problem or "C" client, and place a check in Column 2b if it is a "D" or truly undesirable client.
3. List the fees generated during the previous 12 months in Column 3a and the percentage of total fees represented by each (refer to Figure

3–1 for this data) in Column 3b. Estimate the fees to be received during the next 12 months in Column 3c.

4. Place a "Yes" in Column 4 if the client is to be classified as a target of attention due to warning signals that suggest the financial picture is negative.

"C" clients are often created the moment the professional caves in while discussing fees and collection policies during preliminary business meetings with prospective clients.

DROP THE "D"s

Too often marginal clients receive "A" level attention, and, as a result, key clients may be neglected. Your three action steps are clear: (1) look for those few clients whom you can educate and influence to change and upgrade to a "B," (2) realistically identify those relatively few problem clients you *must* keep because of previous commitments, and (3) identify candidates for termination. For every five "D" (or possibly "C") hours terminated, you'll gain hours more energy and enjoyment.

A "D" client is often created when the professional accedes on a matter of policy. During a seminar conducted for a group of managing partners of actuarial firms, we examined the anatomy of a "D" client and realized that such a client is often educated to behave in this manner.

One possible solution to "D" clients involves analysis of the cause(s) of this particular client situation. The professional should accept responsibility for the situation and reeducate the client, pointing out that conditions have changed. The relationship must then be renegotiated.

PAY ATTENTION TO THE "U"s

Your goal is to classify every client as soon as you can so you can take the appropriate next steps. Make every client currently designated as "U" a target of attention for the next 12 months, during which time you will assign it the appropriate client classification code.

ASSESSMENT PAYS OFF

If you're like most professionals, you have probably never assessed and listed your clients in the manner described in this chapter. Yet, after doing so, you'll readily see that assessment of the present client base is essential for understanding the nature of your practice and for beginning to develop a framework for attracting more "A" and "B" clients.

CHAPTER 5

Assessing Your Current Prospective Clients

Prospective clients are nonclient organizations, associations, and individuals with whom you have had a serious discussion about the possibility of providing a service. Because of their importance, they are automatically designated as targets of opportunity.

After completing the actions recommended in this brief chapter, you will be able to:

☐ Identify current prospective clients who are in your potential new business pipeline.

☐ Determine the potential new revenue they represent.

☐ Estimate the probability of converting them into desirable new clients.

☐ Devise a plan for converting them into desirable new clients.

YOUR FUTURE IS IN YOUR HANDS

The number and quality of your current prospective clients determines to a large extent what your future practice will look like. Your goal at all times is to keep your potential new business pipeline full and flowing.

Let's look at the prospective clients you have on hand who can be

FIGURE 5–1
Current Prospective Clients

1	2	3	4	5
Organization/ Individual's Name	Contact's Name and Title	SIC #	Date of First Contact	Proposed Service Solution

converted into new clients. The subject of prospecting will be covered fully in Chapter 24.

   Figure 5–1 is a convenient form to use in making an inventory of your current prospective clients. The instructions for preparing this form are as follows:

1. List the name of the prospective client in Column 1.

2. List the primary contact's name and title in Column 2.

3. Enter the four-digit SIC number in Column 3.

4. List the date of initial contact in Column 4. This is important because you want to keep track of the age of each prospect. Unlike a good wine, prospects seldom get better with age.

5. Describe the proposed service(s) solution in Column 5.

6. Enter the estimated fee in Column 6.

7. Determine if this is a short-term opportunity, and if yes, place a

6	7	8	
	Short-Term Opportunity	Plan for Conversion	
Estimated Fee		a. What?	b. When?
$_____			

"Yes" in Column 6. This opportunity is recorded in the targets of opportunity section of your personal marketing plan, which is discussed in Chapter 27.

8. Describe your plan for converting each prospect into a desirable new client:

- List the next steps you will take in Column 8a, "What?"
- List when you will do each step in Column 8b.

Figure 5–1 is a powerful marketing tool. You'll be glad you prepared such an inventory for your practice because it lets you focus on the must-do actions required to bring profitable new clients into your practice.

With this important step behind us, let's move to Chapter 6 and assess your financial performance.

CHAPTER 6

Assessing Your Financial Performance

This chapter's sole purpose is to emphasize that benchmarks and indicators of previous performance are needed to enable you to move in a more prosperous direction—you have to know where you've been and where you're going.

A three-year period is used to eliminate seasonal, cyclical, and unusual fluctuations, such as providing an unusually large amount of special services to several of your largest clients.

A THREE-YEAR REVIEW

To complete this chapter you will need to obtain the following data for the latest 36 months (or if you've been in business for less than 36 months, for as long as you've been in practice):

☐ Total fees you personally billed

☐ Billable client work (number of hours you personally invested)

☐ Marketing and practice development (again, your hours)

☐ Other activities

☐ Information on clients acquired/lost

YOUR PERSONAL
BILLING PERFORMANCE

Figure 6–1 can be used to record your *personal* billing performance. In working with this simple form, you can round the numbers to the nearest thousand, and the percent to the nearest whole number.

PERFORMANCE TREND?

Does your three-year performance profile suggest a trend or pattern? Does it meet your expectations?

If your situation indicates real growth, can you recruit and retain the staff you need? And are you:

1. Working harder and reaping more rewards?

2. Managing more and personally billing less?

3. Keeping pace with or outrunning other partners, practices, and inflation?

If your situation indicates a decline, are you surprised? Is it within tolerance limits? Are you aware of the reasons for the decline?

What can you conclude from this simple analysis? You may now wish to complete this analysis for other professionals in your firm (if applicable).

FIGURE 6–1
Personal Billing Performance

Year	Revenue, $	Growth, %
19XX	_____	_____
19XX	_____	_____
19XX	_____	_____
19XX	_____	_____
19XX	_____	_____
19XX	_____	_____

FIGURE 6–2
Personal Hourly Performance

Activity Areas	19XX	19XX	19XX
Chargeable client work	_____	_____	_____
Marketing and practice development	_____	_____	_____
Other activities	══════	══════	══════
Total	_____	_____	_____

YOUR DISTRIBUTION OF PERSONAL HOURS

Figure 6–2 can be used to list your personal *hourly* data. The numbers here tell an important story, so be accurate in listing them in each category.

Does your three-year profile suggest a trend or pattern? Does it meet your personal goals? You may find it useful to construct your own chart or spreadsheet to facilitate a more detailed financial analysis.

The important point is that you must establish benchmarks for billing rate, revenue growth, and distribution of personal hours to effectively critique previous performance and establish new, desirable performance goals.

YOUR CLIENT "CHURN" PICTURE

The last financial factor for assessment is the nature of your client "churn," the number and dollar value of and reason for clients acquired or lost.

Figure 6–3 can be reproduced and used to identify:

1. The number of clients acquired for each year.

2. The source of clients acquired.

3. The dollar value of clients acquired.

4. The number of clients lost each year.

5. The reason for the losses.

6. The dollar value of clients lost.

FIGURE 6–3
Clients Acquired/Lost Profile

Start Date _____			Present Date _____		
Clients Acquired			Clients Lost		
Source	Number	Fees	Reasons	Number	Fees
Client referrals	_____	$ _____	Work completed	_____	$ _____
Leads from recommendations	_____	$ _____	Fee complaint	_____	$ _____
Drop-ins/image	_____	$ _____	Service complaint	_____	$ _____
Targeted, self-initiated action	_____	$ _____	Moved out of market	_____	$ _____
Advertising	_____	$ _____	Merger or acquisition	_____	$ _____
Unknown	_____	$ _____	Bankruptcy	_____	$ _____
			Outside pressure Bank Government	_____ _____	$ _____ $ _____
			Sale of business	_____	$ _____
			Unknown	_____	$ _____
Totals	_____	$ _____	Totals	_____	$ _____

Review Figure 6–3 carefully because it shows the strength of the sources of new clients, and the severity of the reasons for losing clients. This figure reveals a picture of the health of your practice. With this information at hand, you have a clear picture of the marketing and client retention job ahead of you.

We turn next to determining your current industry-market niches, an important leveraging step that results in positioning your practice for profitability.

CHAPTER 7

Assessing Your Current and Potential Niches

The purpose of this chapter is to expand your horizons in the assessment of present and potential industry-market niches that you can systematically penetrate, and, hopefully, dominate in the future. The information and work sheets that follow provide you with the knowledge and tools to select niches with potential for profitable, sustained growth, and will enable you to answer these questions:

☐ What is a primary industry-market niche?

☐ Why is it important to select such niches?

☐ What are *your* current primary niches, and how much potential does each have?

☐ What human sources of information will enable you to learn about new niches?

☐ What printed sources of information will enable you to learn about new niches?

☐ How can you inexpensively research new potential niches?

A BRIEF REVIEW OF MUST-KNOW FUNDAMENTALS

In Chapter 1 we defined an industry as an SIC grouping of organizations and individuals that address the same needs of their clients and customers through the delivery of their goods and services. A market is designated by the postal ZIPs in your practice area. Taken together, your SIC–ZIP combinations are called *niches*.

A niche is composed of clients, prospective clients, and "suspects," nonclients in your practice area you have not yet contacted. A niche also contains nonclient influentials who impact and influence the hiring decisions of your targets of opportunity in each niche.

The niches you serve represent different potential for your practice:

1. A *primary* niche is one in which the revenues produced by all your clients in the SIC constitute a large percentage of your total revenue.

2. A *secondary* niche is one in which the current revenue produced by all of your clients in the SIC constitutes a small percentage of your total revenue.

YOUR CONTINUING GOAL

Your continuing goal is to identify high-potential niches and execute effective action programs designed to penetrate them by offering solution programs meeting hot-button needs with high-margin service solutions.

FIGURE 3–1 REVISITED

In Chapter 3 you were asked to prepare a data input work sheet, which enabled you to list and process important data about your current clients. You were asked to compute the total dollar value and percentage of total estimated potential fees within each SIC and to array them from largest to smallest.

Now you are ready to use the analysis in one of your most important marketing decisions: selecting one or more niches for focused attention, as targets of opportunity. Figure 7–1 is a convenient form for your use in making niching decisions. To use this form to its fullest:

1. Enter the four-digit SIC number of your current niches from the largest percentage of total revenue to the smallest. Place the SICs with largest percentages in the primary niche section.

2. Define the niche (paving and roofing materials, for example) on the line calling for a description of the niche.

3. Estimate the potential for growth for your firm both in the short term, within 12 months, and long term, beyond 12 months, using an "H" for high potential, an "M" for moderate potential, and "L" for low potential.

FIGURE 7–1
Current Primary and Secondary Niches

Current Primary Niches

	SIC Number	% Total Revenue	Description of Niche	Potential for Growth* Short-Term**	Long-Term***
1.	( )				
2.	( )				
3.	( )				
4.	( )				
5.	( )				
6.	( )				
7.	( )				
8.	( )				

Current Secondary Niches

	SIC Number	% Total Revenue	Description of Niche	Potential for Growth* Short-Term**	Long-Term***
1.	( )				
2.	( )				
3.	( )				
4.	( )				
5.	( )				
6.	( )				
7.	( )				
8.	( )				

*List an H, M, or L
**Short-term = now up to 12 months
***Long-term = beyond 12 months

TAKE A PENETRATING LOOK AT YOUR CURRENT NICHES

As you review the results of your completed form, thoughtfully consider and answer the question: "Are these primary niches the ones I should or want to be in?" If not, determine any secondary niches that warrant your attention for analysis, planning, and action, for these have now become your targets of opportunity.

After attending one of Dick's niching seminars, a professional profiled her practice by determining the percentage of total and projected fees for each of her current primary niches. Then she used the various research documents available to target industries to estimate the potential for industry growth, and for growth of her types of services. She did this by talking with other suppliers of business and professional services who targeted this niche. After telephoning directors of several associations comprised of member firms who were both clients and targets, she confirmed her suspicion that she had indeed selected a "rich niche" for targeting.

WHAT ABOUT OTHER NICHES?

In examining other niches, inexpensively, you may wish to consult your key clients, industry associates, studies, analysts, and stockbrokers.

However, whether you are a one-person service firm or part of an internationally established firm, you can generate nearly instantaneous data in every level of scope and depth on any target niche from individuals and households to the largest Fortune 500 and multinational firms. Every public and college library contains a host of comprehensive, annually updated directories. Here are several examples from the several hundred available.

The International Directory of Company Histories. Published by St. James Press based in Chicago, Illinois, and London, England, provides detailed and historical information on 1,250 of the world's largest and most influential companies in five volumes of 250 entries each. Information on each company includes the mailing address, phone number, public or private ownership, state controlled or not, incorporation date, number of employees, sales and market value, and stock index. All five volumes exceed 3,500 pages.

Europe's 5,000 Largest Companies. Published annually by R.R. Bowker in New York, provides financial data on the 500 largest industrial and 1,000 largest trading companies throughout Europe. Offers different rankings of industrials by profit, volume, and various other measures.

Canadian Business. Offers "2 + 2: the top 200, plus the next 200 of Canada's largest companies" each year in the July issue. Published by C.B. Media, Ltd., Toronto, Ontario.

Corporate Technology Directory. Published by CorpTech located in Wellesley Hills, Massachusetts, provides the names of 26,000 companies including 15,100 emerging private companies. Also lists 7,800 key executives and 86,000 high-tech products. The publication, more than 4,000 pages, is contained in four volumes.

Findex. Identifies more than 1,200 research reports in 12 categories including business and finance, health care, consumer durables, consumer nondurables, defense and security systems, media, and publishing. Also energy, utilities, and related equipment; data processing systems and electronic equipment; construction materials and machinery; basic industries and related equipment; retailer and consumer services; and transportation.

U.S. Manufacturers Directory. Published by American Business Directories, it lists more than 200,000 U.S. manufacturers by company name, address, zip code, and phone number and offers data on number of employees, sales volume, names of owner, manager, and chief executive officer, and up to three SIC codes per company. It is cross-indexed by city and state, type of industry, and number of employees.

EMPLOYING DATA BASES

Articles, abstracts, briefs, and industry reports, all of which are provided by data bases, can give you key information on the operational characteristics of targeted markets. Vendors offering a wide selection of data bases include Lockheed Dialog, SDC Orbit, Business Retrieval System, and Mead Data Central. These systems offer several hundred data bases from which to gather information on any market.

INDEXES

Jeff's clients often ask if there is a quick way to collect information on prospects via magazines and newspapers. The *Magazine Index* and *Newspaper Index* in the United States offer comprehensive bibliographies of articles in microfiche. If you seek an article or information that appeared in your local newspaper on a particular market, use the library's newspaper index, which abstracts newspaper articles by topic and cross-references this listing by date. Large metro areas are often served by one or more area business publications. Write to the Association of Area Business Publications, 202 Legion Drive, Annapolis, MD 21401, for a list of hundreds of area business publications. Also, *The Wall Street Journal Index* is available in many public libraries in major cities.

Most U.S. public libraries maintain a copy of the *Business Periodicals Index*, the *Reader's Guide to Periodical Literature*, and the *Reader's*

Guide to Scientific Literature. You may scan these indices for the latest articles in selected industry areas. For example, using the *Business Periodicals Index*, you can obtain the listing of all the articles in the last month, quarter, year, or 50 years, appearing in such nationally known business journals as *Business Week, Fortune, Forbes,* and *The Harvard Business Review,* as well as numerous other business periodicals.

Your public library also maintains a generous supply of telephone directories for both your geographic area and major cities across North America. These serve as good starting points for identifying clients.

Association directories can be found in any library and offer the names, addresses, and telephone numbers of industry, trade, and professional associations. Two directories in particular—*Gales Encyclopedia of Associations,* and *National Trade and Professional Associations*—collectively offer over 10,000 association listings. The associations themselves can provide industry trend information, surveys, publications, and many other services.

An advertising agency in Tulsa, Oklahoma, was able to identify hundreds of medium-size retailers in its local area by obtaining a directory published by a state retail trade association.

If you wish to identify a specific or perhaps obscure industry or trade journal, consult Urich's *International Guide to Periodicals, Working Press of the Nation, Writer's Market, Bacon's Publicity Checker,* or the *Standard Periodicals Directory*. These directories are updated annually and collectively contain listings of over 12,000 technical and trade publications. By purchasing the subscription list of *Engineering News Record,* a graphic design firm in Minneapolis obtained dozens of new business leads through an effective direct mail campaign.

Suppliers' guides, often called *blue books* or *red books,* can be found in the business reference section of many public libraries. For example, the *Blue Book of Metro Area Home Builders* and *Red Book of Plumbing Supply Contractors* (representative, not actual titles) might be distributed by the local associations serving these industries.

Thomas' Register and *Cahners Buyer's Guide* contain a wealth of information on durable goods suppliers and can be used as target market lists.

FEDERAL GOVERNMENT INFORMATION SOURCES

The U.S. government is one of the largest publishers in the world. Through the Bureau of Census of the Department of Commerce, you may obtain sales and revenue data on virtually any industry by state, county, and standard metropolitan statistical area. Although the Bureau of Census is known primarily for its population reports, a census of business is taken on the second and seventh year of each decade and is generally available 18 to 24 months thereafter. The Bureau of Census also produces many special industry reports and offers several ways to access their files. The Bureau of the Census, as well as the U.S. Department of Commerce and the U.S. Department of Agriculture, for example, publish a wide variety of market and industry reports on regions throughout the world. To obtain a list of the bureau's publications, write to

> Public Information Office
> Bureau of the Census
> Department of Commerce
> Washington, DC 20233
> (301) 763–4051

The Department of Commerce also produces the *U.S. Industrial Outlook,* which traces the growth of 200 industries and provides five-year forecasts for each industry. The *U.S. Statistical Abstract* is a compilation of data and reports from the Department of Commerce, the Department of Labor, the Department of Transportation, the Small Business Administration, and other federal agencies. The *Statistical Abstract* is particularly useful because it contains over 800 charts and graphs.

If you need to access information within a specific federal government agency, it is best to call the Public Information Office rather than the agency switchboard. When trying to identify a specific individual, ask for the Locator's Office, and when trying to identify a specific nonclassified document, use the Freedom of Information Office.

Many of the major publications produced by the federal government are on sale at the U.S. Government Printing Office. For a free catalog, write to:

> Superintendent of Documents
> U.S. Government Printing Office
> Washington, DC 20401

The federally sponsored National Technical Information Service (NTIS) maintains abstracts and data bases in 28 technical areas, such as engineering and energy. Descriptive brochures may be obtained by writing to

> National Technical Information Service
> Department of Commerce
> 5285 Port Royal Road
> Springfield, Virginia 22161
> (703) 487–4600

Remember, if you are a U.S. taxpayer, you have already paid for many of the federal government information sources that have been established. Use them!

STATE GOVERNMENT INFORMATION SOURCES

Nearly all of the 50 states have their own Department of Commerce, many have their own Department of Energy, and a few have special small business offices. The state capital, the state capital library, the governor's office, and the offices of your elected representatives often maintain special reports, studies, and analyses that may prove useful in your research efforts.

On a regional or local basis, various planning committees, the Chamber of Commerce, the research department of newspapers, highway commissions, local libraries, and the county courthouse are just a few of the information sources you may wish to tap. Many professionals have found that a wealth of information can be gained over the telephone or by simply visiting nearby organizations or agencies.

Internationally, virtually every country has a department of commerce or trade, and most have development and export/import liaison offices.

PUBLISHERS

Several key publishers, including Gale Press, Book Tower, Detroit, MI 48226; Facts on File, 460 Park Avenue South, New York, NY 10016; and John Wiley & Sons, 605 Third Avenue, New York, NY 10158 offer free catalogs listing numerous information directories that they publish. The Gale Press, for example, offers a directory of consultants and consulting organizations, a guide to research centers, and even a directory of directories.

NEWSLETTERS

Newsletters are a valuable source of research information. Newsletters are now published by all industry groups and major associations. The *Oxbridge Newsletter Directory* lists several thousand newsletters, arranged by functional area. *National Trade and Professional Associations* indicates which, of the thousands of associations listed, maintain a newsletter. By accessing these directories and others suggested by your local librarian, you can gain access to valuable, inside information related to new primary markets. Many newsletters are read religiously by their subscribers. If you read what your target market reads, then you can more readily serve that market.

The ability to effectively gather valuable information is directly related to how organized you are. It may be necessary to befriend information sources such as librarians, publishers, and federal agency representatives because you will often have the need to call on these people more than once.

The assessment technique and research methodologies discussed in this chapter have been specifically geared to the professional who does not have the resources to undertake exhaustive research efforts. Once you or your staff have become familiar with the reference sources cited, the task of generating timely effective research information will become easier.

CHAPTER 8

Sizing Up Your Services

The services you offer and provide to your clients and prospective clients must be perceived as adding value to the operations of the buyer. In this chapter we'll examine your services from two important viewpoints.

After completing the exercises in this chapter you will be able to:

☐ Prepare a profile of your current services to determine the attractiveness of each service to your desirable clients.

☐ Determine which services are to be designated as targets of attention.

☐ Prepare a client-centered service analysis which you will use in personal selling contacts and in preparing promotional materials.

PREPARING YOUR CURRENT SERVICES PROFILE

Figure 8–1 provides you with a practical form for assessing the nature and scope of your current services. Using this form requires that you:

1. Rank your services from the largest revenues to the smallest revenues during the most recent 12 months, and list each service by name in Column 1.

FIGURE 8–1
Current Services Profile

	1	2	3
	Services	*Fees from Services*	*% of Total Fees*
1.	_____	$	%
2.	_____	$	%
3.	_____	$	%
4.	_____	$	%
5.	_____	$	%
6.	_____	$	%
7.	_____	$	%
8.	_____	$	%
9.	_____	$	%
10.	_____	$	%
11.	_____	$	%
12.	_____	$	%
	Total Fees	$	100%

Class I = Needed and not wanted
Class II = Needed and wanted

2. List all the fees obtained from each service in Column 2.

3. Compute the total fees and determine the percentage of total fees from each service. Enter this percentage in Column 3.

4. Determine whether each service can be classified as *leading edge, competitive,* or *falling behind* in terms of technology, client acceptance, and your interest in providing it. Place an "X" in the appropriate column under the analysis designation in Column 4a, 4b, or 4c.

5. Determine whether each service is seen as a Class I or Class II service by your clients and prospective clients, and place an "X" in the appropriate column under the designation Class, in Column 5a or 5b.

6. Jot your comments and implications ideas in Column 6.

4 Analysis			5 Class		6
Leading Edge	Compe- titive	Falling Behind	a. I	b. II	Comments/ Implications

You've now completed an important analysis of your services. In general, you want to be able to position your services as Class II leading edge solutions to important needs and problems. Services that you deem necessary for continued survival of your practice, but are perceived by clients as falling behind in terms of technology and attractiveness, need to be classified as targets of attention, and the appropriate level of attention and resources allocated to them.

DEVELOPING A CLIENT-CENTERED VIEW OF YOUR SERVICES

Now let's develop a client-centered view of the services you provide. The insights developed as a result of this analysis will serve you well in selling additional services to your clients and prospective clients. The understanding will also be useful in preparing written promotional and proposal-related documents.

FIGURE 8–2
Client-Centered Service Analysis

For: _____
                                    (Service)

Your task is to identify client needs and problem situations for which your service is appropriate. For each verb listed below, identify how your service applies. For example, under the word "eliminate" you might put "unnecessary forms and procedures."

Improve or Enhance	Reduce, Relieve, or Eliminate
Protect	**Restructure**
Identify	**Restore or Resolve**

A professional service is largely an intangible idea that is purchased for the end results it will produce. As stated previously, clients don't really purchase services; they purchase the expectations of receiving a more favorable future. The future contains expected *benefits* to the purchaser.

Benefits exist solely in the perception of the client. Benefits are always related to the client's needs and expectations about the way in which those needs and expectations will be met.

Figure 8–2, "Client-Centered Service Analysis," can be used to identify benefits that are important to clients and, indeed, to force you to view services as your clients and prospective clients perceive them.

To use the form effectively, follow these steps:

1. Enter the name of the service you want to analyze on the top line.

2. Move to the upper left-hand block, "Improve or Enhance," and ask: "In what ways does this service enable purchasers or users to improve or enhance something they value?" List your answers in the block—for example, "improve market penetration," "enhance image," and so on.

3. Move next to the upper right-hand block and ask: "In what ways does this service reduce, relieve, or eliminate some unwanted condition?" List your answers in the block—for example, "reduce filing time," "relieve backlog pressures," and so forth.

4. Move to the "Protect" block and ask: "In what ways does this service enable the purchaser or users to protect something they value?" Again, list your answers in the block.

5. Then move to the remaining blocks and complete them in a similar manner.

Note: Not all blocks need to be or will be completed for a given service.

You now have a set of potential benefits that can accrue to a client. The completed chart can be used in proposal writing and face-to-face discussions with clients and training staff.

Other key service words and phrases that could be used in filling out the client-centered service analysis are as follows:

Improve

Decision-making capability	Understanding of costs
Profits	Appearance
Cash flow position	Information for decisions
Through-put time	Credit rating
Internal operations	User service needs
Public product image	Long-term outlook
Quality, reliability, effectiveness of software	Competitive capabilities
	Employee morale and motivation
Usefulness and relevance of documentation	Employee safety
	Market position
Operating efficiency and productivity	Use of EOP equipment

Enhance

Credibility of client's role in
    community
User orientation of software
Service to particular groups or
    users
Inherent advantages
Shareholder value
Competitive edge
Utilization of equipment and
    facilities

Employee morale and motivation
Working capital position
Organizational image
Technical understanding of
    problem
Existing strengths and image
Status in peer group
Existing skills
Multinational marketing
    opportunities

Reduce

Number of internal and external
    conflicts
Costs
Deficits
Downtime
Skills levels requirements
Service delays and unreliability

Excess capacity
Idle equipment time
Peaking of demands
Risk
Waste
Inefficiency
Tax liabilities

Relieve

Conflict
Congestion
Public pressure and adverse
    opinions
Recurring problems

Future cost pressures
Pressure and tension
Organization conflicts
Blockages to staff development
Undue workload

Eliminate

Inefficiencies and waste
Bottlenecks
Misappropriation of resources
Conflict
Constraints
Headache
Adverse criticism
Low cost-benefit ratios

Extra paperwork
Deficits
Cumbersome routines
Pilferage and internal security
    problems
Shortsightedness
Unnecessary cost

Protect

Client reputation and integrity
Independence
Assets
Market position and market share

Security of product served
Proprietary information
Integrity and public image
Self-interests

Restructure

Organization
Current operations
Work flow
Planning process
Reporting systems

Compensation and incentive
 program
Operating mechanisms
Internal operations

Identify

Strategies
Key problem areas
Decision factors
Unforeseen opportunities
Solutions to problem areas
Needs

Available resources
Alternatives or options
Constraints or limits
Market shifts
Potentials

Restore and Revitalize

Profitable operations
Role of organization in
 community
Standardized development process
Deteriorating facilities and
 equipment
Long-term outlook

Markets, competitive edge, and
 profits
Management structure
Employee morale—motivation
Market penetration
Outdated skills
Cash flow position

A sample of how an accountant might complete Figure 8–2 for an audit service is presented in Figure 8–3.

With this important chapter behind us, let's move now into an examination of your referral sources.

FIGURE 8–3
Completed Client-Centered Service Analysis

For: AUDIT SERVICES
_____
(Service)

Your task is to identify client needs and problem situations for which your service is appropriate. For each verb listed below, identify how your service applies. For example, under the word "eliminate" you might put "unnecessary forms and procedures."

Improve or Enhance	Reduce, Relieve, or Eliminate
Cash flow	Exposure to loss
Profitability	Paperwork
Accounting procedures	Bottlenecks
Operations	Investment debt
Revenues	Material errors
Internal control	Errors
Internal reporting	
Protect	**Restructure**
Assets	Quality of reporting system
Credibility	Unprofitable operations
Reputation	Unnecessary reports
Profit	Branch operations
Lines of credit	
Liquidity	
Develop or Install	**Restore or Resolve**
External reporting	Image of client
Management information system	Reliability of financial statements
Cost systems	Resolve backlogs, uncertainty, inefficiencies, management anxiety
Decision-making model	

CHAPTER 9

Cultivating Your Existing Referral Sources

Creating and maintaining strong and active referral relationships is an essential client-centered marketing task that effectively leverages your new business production time. A targeted referrals program is the backbone of a successful practice. Yet, too many professionals regard this as a burdensome, or worse, unimportant task.

This chapter discusses identification, education, retention, and leveraging your relationships with those desirable clients and nonclients who make referrals and introductions and provide you with new business leads. This chapter provides the answers to these questions:

☐ What are the benefits of building a referrals program?

☐ What are the two classes of referral sources?

☐ How can each type of referral be used to best advantage?

☐ What is the best way to inventory and analyze your current referral sources?

☐ What is the best way to show appreciation for the efforts made by your referral sources?

☐ How do you best leverage your current referral sources?

PAYOFFS FROM REFERRAL BUILDING

Building and maintaining an active referral program produces several key benefits and makes your marketing task easier because it enables you to:

- Make contacts with preconditioned prospective clients who are generally more receptive to meeting with you because of their regard for the referral person.
- Acquire an insider's understanding of their industry/profession because you have the opportunity to discuss changes, trends, and needs in their area of operations.
- Develop additional business contacts while working within your comfort zone. This eliminates much of the resistance that is often encountered in other more aggressive marketing approaches.

TWO CLASSES OF REFERRAL SOURCES

There are two different classes of referrals: existing and former clients, who make referrals in your behalf, and nonclient influentials. Each referral source has distinct benefits and requirements for development.

TRACKING YOUR CURRENT CLIENT REFERRAL SOURCES

Figure 9–1 is a convenient form you can use to keep track of your current "A" clients who make referrals in your behalf. Refer to Figure 4–2 on page 22 for the names of your current client referral sources. Now:

1. Transfer the names of current clients with a "Yes" in Column 2 of Figure 4–2 to Column 1 of Figure 9–1.
2. Classify the type of referral source they represent. Do they initiate leads and referrals, or are they the more passive vouch-for types?
   a. If they do not initiate leads and referrals, place an "X" in the No Column after their name.
   b. If you designate them as "Yes" for being initiators, list the level of effort they invest in your behalf in the Yes column of Column 2. Keeping a record of the frequency of their referrals is an important step.
      - An "A" in the initiate column means that this client is a continuing/recurring referral source.
      - A "B" means that they are a sporadic source.
      - A "C" means that they are or have been a one-time-only referral source.

FIGURE 9–1
Existing Client Referral Sources

1	2		3	4		5
	Initiate?		Quality of	Potential**		
Client Executives Name and Affiliation	No	Yes*	Relationship (1 to 4)	Short-Term	Long-Term	How I Plan to Use This Referral Source

*Level of effort	1 = Poor	**Potential
A = continuing/recurring	4 = Perfect	H = High
B = sporadic		M = Medium
C = one time only/dormant		L = Low

3. Assess the current quality of relationship with each client. Using a scale of 1, which is a poor relationship, up to 4, which is a perfect relationship, assign the proper number to each, and place this number in Column 3. Any relationship assessed a 2 or 1 automatically becomes a target of attention.

4. Estimate the potential for providing referrals both in the short term, within 12 months, and long term, beyond 12 months, using an "H" for high potential, "M" for medium potential, and "L" for low potential. Put the appropriate letters in the short-term and long-term columns of Column 4.

5. Complete the form by spelling out in detail how you plan to use this valued referral source. This information will be used later as you build your personal marketing plan.

Assessing Your Current Client Referrals

Once your inventory is complete, you will want to consider the following questions:

- How many of my "A" clients, of the total "A"s I serve, actually make referrals at this time?

- Why don't more of my "A" clients make referrals?
- How many initiators have I created?
- How frequently do I thank my sources?
- Do all my "A" clients know I am interested in obtaining their leads? Or do I look too busy to handle more work?
- Which referral sources are drying up and why?

TRACKING YOUR CURRENT NONCLIENT REFERRAL SOURCES

Nonclient influentials are attorneys, bankers, noncompeting consultants, and others who serve and influence your targeted clients and prospective clients. There are four classes of nonclient influentials:

1. *Reciprocals*—other noncompeting professionals serving your targeted prospective clients. These valuable relationships provide you with leads and introductions and expect you to provide them with leads and to mention them to your contacts as appropriate.

2. *Niche multipliers*—people who serve your targeted niches and have the potential to influence large numbers of your targets in your behalf. The best sources of multipliers are executive directors of associations serving the niches, editors of publications read by members of the niche, and current movers-and-shakers in the niche.

3. *Market/community multipliers*—people who come into contact with your targets of opportunity (prospective clients) and can provide you with leads and mention your name when appropriate.

4. *Personal influentials*—your friends, college alumni, alumni of your firm, etc.

Figure 9–2 should be used to list the names of your nonclient influentials, such as the following:

Accountants	Attorneys
Politicians	Editors
Alumni of your firm	Board members
Bankers and investment bankers	Peers
Association executives	Industry leaders
Insurance agents	Other influentials

Now, in completing Figure 9–2:

1. In the first column, list the names and affiliations of your influential contacts.

FIGURE 9–2
Existing Nonclient Influentials

1	2		3	4		5
Names and Affiliations of Influential Contacts	Initiate?		Quality of Relationship (1 to 4)	Potential**		How I Plan to Use This Referral Source
	No	Yes*		Short-Term	Long-Term	

*Level of effort   1 = Low   **Potential
A = continuing/recurring   4 = Perfect   H = High
B = sporadic   M = Medium
C = one time only/dormant   L = Low

2. Classify the type of referral made. Do they initiate leads and referrals, or are they the more passive vouch-for types?

3. If you designate them as "Yes" for being initiators, next list the level of effort they invest in your behalf. Keeping a record of the frequency of their referrals is an important step. An "A" in the initiate column means that this influential contact is a continuing/recurring referral source. A "B" means that they are a sporadic source, and a "C" means that they are or have been a one-time-only referral source.

4. Assess the current quality of relationship with each influential contact. Using a scale of 1, which is a poor relationship, up to 4 which is a perfect relationship, assign the proper number for each. Any relationship assessed a 2 or 1 automatically becomes a target of attention.

5. Estimate the potential for providing referrals both in the short term, within 12 months, and long term, beyond 12 months, using an "H" for high potential, "M" for medium potential, and "L" for low potential.

6. Complete the form by spelling out in detail how you plan to use this valued referral source. This information will be used later as you build your personal marketing plan.

Assessing Your Current Nonclient Influentials

Once your inventory is complete, you will want to consider the following questions:

1. How many influential relationships, such as attorneys and bankers, do I have in each category?

2. What makes these particular individuals influential? Why do they provide me with leads?

3. What is the quality of my relationship with key influential associates?

4. How frequently do I contact these influentials to thank them for their efforts and seek additional leads?

5. How frequently do I reciprocate by making appropriate referrals to them?

After answering these questions, many professionals find that they have been lax in the cultivation and maintenance of referrals.

For years a top partner in a law firm had obtained leads from the lending officer in a prestigious bank. He became complacent, however, and admittedly took the referral source for granted—he lengthened the time between contact and increasingly neglected to send follow-up thank you notes or to provide feedback to the lending officer. One day the partner realized that this once fertile referral source had dried up. To this day, he has been unable to turn the flow of leads back on.

If you find yourself in the lax category, why not resolve now to begin an aggressive campaign to develop and cultivate referral sources?

THANK YOU, THANK YOU

After you have identified all client and nonclient referral sources, your next mission is to acknowledge your referral sources' assistance to you and to "educate" them about the kind of new client(s) and/or market(s) you are best able to serve. Ask referral sources for introductions to industry and/or market opinion leaders and so on. People generally like to assist others who have a sense of purpose and gratitude.

In the next chapter we examine your current targets of opportunity, attention, and influence.

PART THREE

Determining Your Targets: Leveraging in Action

Part Three enables you to focus your attention on the must-do factors in your practice. In this part you will identify your current targets of opportunity, targets of attention, and targets of influence, and determine immediate next steps you will list in your personal marketing plan.

Upon conclusion of this part you will have determined where you should best focus your resources and time during the next marketing period. We suggest that you invest sufficient time in this essential task.

CHAPTER 10

Working with Your Targets of Opportunity

This chapter begins to bring the results of your previous marketing tasks together. You've completed the data input and analysis, you've classified your clients, and now you are ready to leverage your time, talents, and technology as you work with your targets of opportunity.

This chapter will provide answers to the following questions:

☐ How do I identify my current targets of opportunity?

☐ How do I best capitalize on them?

☐ What should be my continuing goal with my targets of opportunity?

☐ How do I build marketing into my work processes?

Your targets of opportunity include:

- Current "A" and "B" clients with needs about which to be contacted during the current planning action period (the 90-day period covered by your personal marketing plan).

- Prospective clients that represent potential for generating additional revenues in the period.

- Current "C" clients with potential for positive fee adjustments during the period.

ORGANIZING FOR TARGETING

Please assemble the following materials:

1. Completed Figure 4–2 (page 22), "Existing "A" Clients"
2. Completed Figure 4–4 (page 26), "Existing "B" Clients"
3. Completed Figure 5–1 (page 32), "Current Prospective Clients"
4. The blank form for Figure 27–2 (page 204), "Personal Marketing Plan," which you will begin to fill in.

IDENTIFYING YOUR CURRENT TARGETS OF OPPORTUNITY

Refer to Figure 4–2, which lists your existing "A" clients, and Figure 27–2, which is the "shell" of your personal marketing plan for the current planning-action period.

Look first at Column 6 on Figure 4–2. Transfer the names of all the clients listed there as opportunity clients to Section 1, "Targets of Opportunity," on the personal marketing plan as follows. First list the names of the opportunity clients having an "H" letter code in Column 3 on Figure 4–2, then those with an "M" and, finally those with an "L." You now have a list of "A" clients with known or suspected needs who are to be contacted during the period.

Turn now to Figure 4–4. Look first at Column 6. Transfer the names of clients listed there as opportunity clients to Section 1, "Targets of Opportunity," on the personal marketing plan. List first the "B" opportunity clients having an "H" letter code, then those with an "M," and finally those with an "L" as you did with Figure 4–2. You now have a list of "B" clients with known or suspected needs who are to be contacted during the next period.

Turn next to Figure 5–1, which contains your list of current prospective clients. Look at Column 8b, the "When?" portion of your conversion plan. List the name of each prospective client you plan to contact during the current period in the targets of opportunity section of the plan.

Finally, list the names of the few "C" clients that warrant your attention, for example because you feel it is now possible to remove or reduce any fee adjustment you made in order to do, obtain, or retain their business.

The "when" of your work steps should be realistically scheduled. Don't make the common mistake of overloading your calendar so that missing one action step scuttles your whole program. Undertake a bit at a time. Win early and often, and celebrate your successes.

EXISTING CLIENTS WITH NEEDS— OPPORTUNITY KNOCKS

Expanding services to existing "A" and "B" clients with needs for your services can be both enjoyable and profitable, and is well within your comfort zone.

Once you have your list of targets of opportunity completed for the period, your next task is to develop and execute a contact program that involves bringing the need to the attention of the client's contact person.

Develop the Positive Point of View

The wrong frame of mind in laying the groundwork for expanding services to your clients is not to sell more services to your targets. Rather, proceed with the mind-set, "In what ways can I assist this client in doing better what she is in business to do?" This client-focused question helps avoid the pushing of your services and builds a sensitivity to being the means to a more favorable future. The how-to's of personal selling will be covered in Chapter 25, but for now your goal should be to enable the client to see that you have solutions to her most pressing needs and problems.

It Should be Your Policy!

The rationale for bringing additional needs to the attention of the client should be established in the first new business meeting you have with a prospective client. For example, tell prospective clients, "It's our service philosophy to be alert to ways in which we can assist you in the conduct of your business. If during the course of the project, we discover any area that we feel needs attention, we'll review our solution programs with you before we complete our work."

Build Marketing into the Engagement Process

A review of your marketing opportunities is particularly appropriate during five engagement phases:

1. *Pre-engagement planning.* Review your files on the client to determine which needs are the current hot-buttons.

2. *Entrance conference.* It's a good idea to review the "Letter of Agreement" with the client at this time. I always mention that I'll be alert to ideas for improvement during the project and will share them at the end of the project.

3. *The engagement.* Be alert to the presence of needs beyond the scope of the current engagement. If you have staff on the engagement,

insist that each prepare a client-need-alert memo that defines an additional known or suspected need to be brought to the attention of the client. Be especially alert to symptoms of needs met by your successful engagements for other similar clients in this industry niche.

4. *End-of-engagement satisfaction meeting.* This is the selling meeting which too few professionals conduct. You begin the meeting by determining the level of client satisfaction with your services. If the reaction is favorable, you obtain referrals and leads and plant the seeds of future need. Properly handled, this meeting will extend into Stage 5.

5. *Post-engagement new business discussion.* During this sales meeting you review the need, identify your proposed solution, discuss procedures, and attempt to convince the client to proceed with your solution program.

CONVERTING YOUR PROSPECTIVE CLIENTS INTO NEW CLIENTS

For each prospect what is your next step? You have two options:

- Send them additional information designed to urge them to proceed. Remind them of the benefits of proceeding, and the costs and consequences of not proceeding.

- Call your contact to see how their decision process is proceeding. A brief call consisting of an "I've been thinking about you and wonder how the decision process is coming along. Any news yet?" is sufficient, although it always pays to mention another benefit.

Eventually you have to make a decision if "Let's proceed" is not forthcoming. Do you drop this contact completely or just put them on "hold" for awhile? We recommend that you ask one more time if there is any chance of proceeding. If "no," Dick asks "Was there something I missed during the proposal process? I really thought there was a fit between your need and my solution." Occasionally a prospect will suggest that the job had been wired (another favored consultant had the inside track) or the situation took a back seat to a more pressing need elsewhere in the organization.

KEEP YOUR TARGETS' PIPELINE FULL
AND FLOWING

Targets of opportunity have a relatively brief shelf life. Your goal should be to constantly monitor the relationships and operations of your "A" clients and high-potential "B" clients for needs and corresponding opportunities for you to help them achieve their goals. This is client-centered service at its finest and tends to generate profitable and recurring revenue.

In the next chapter we'll examine the procedures to be followed in tracking your targets of attention.

Tracking Your Targets of Attention

This chapter discusses the analysis and actions required to successfully capitalize on your targets of attention. Attention is defined as observant or watchful consideration and civility or courtesy. These are two essential attributes of a client-centered approach.

Upon conclusion of this chapter you will be able to:

☐ Identify your current targets of attention.

☐ Determine the best forms of action with your current targets of attention.

☐ Identify warning signals that are evidence of a strain or threat to the primary client-firm relationship.

☐ Employ a four-step client retention plan.

☐ Further leverage your scarce and expensive business development time.

☐ List actions to be taken in your personal marketing plan.

Your targets of attention include the following:

- "A" clients and high-potential "B" clients with "warning signals" in evidence
- "C" and "D" clients giving off warning signals

- "B" clients with potential for upgrading to "A" status
- "U" clients to be classified
- Potential clients to be contacted

ORGANIZING FOR TARGETING

Please assemble the following materials:

1. Partially completed personal marketing plan (Figure 27–2, page 204)
2. Completed Figure 4–2 (page 22), "Existing "A" Clients"
3. Completed Figure 4–4 (page 26), "Existing "B" Clients"
4. Completed Figure 4–5 (page 28), "Existing "C" and "D" Clients"
5. Completed Figure 3–1, (page 18) Data Input Work Sheet

IDENTIFYING YOUR CURRENT TARGETS OF ATTENTION

Refer to Figure 4–2, which lists your existing "A" clients, and Figure 27–2, your partially completed personal marketing plan for the current planning-action period.

Look first at Column 6 on Figure 4–2 and for all the clients listed there as "A" attention clients, transfer their names to Section 2, "Targets of Attention," on the personal marketing plan. You may have another list of "A" clients to be contacted during the period.

Turn now to Figure 4–4. Look first at Column 6 and for clients listed there as "attention clients," transfer their names to the "Targets of Attention" section on the personal marketing plan.

Turn next to Figure 4–5, which contains your list of current "C" and "D" clients. List the name of each client for whom you answered "Yes" to the target of attention question.

Review Figure 3–1 and list the names of all recently acquired clients you classified as "U" on the work sheet in the "Targets of Attention" section of your personal marketing plan.

Finally, list the names of any potential clients you need to contact during the period as part of your prospective activities. Remember, a nonclient becomes a prospective client after you have contacted a nonclient whom you feel meets your minimum acceptance standards. The techniques of prospecting will be discussed later in the book. For now, list the names of potential clients to be contacted this period in the "Targets of Attention" section of your personal marketing plan.

WORKING WITH YOUR TARGETS
OF ATTENTION

The somewhat trite cliche "A stitch in time saves nine!" really applies to your attention situations.

Your fundamental and continuing goal with your "A" clients and "B" clients with potential for upgrading should be to protect and retain the primary client-firm relationship. But situations arise that need to be dealt with. In today's increasingly competitive environment, it's realistic to expect that your most desirable clients are on the targets of attention or targets of opportunity lists of your most aggressive competitors. A light dose of paranoia is a good thing when your good clients are involved. In all cases of dissatisfaction or targeting, it is imperative that you initiate a client retention program.

A Policy You Can Profit From

Figure 11–1 provides a policy statement and checklist that permits you to monitor potential vulnerabilities with existing desirable clients and to remain alert to early warning signals that threaten the relationship. This checklist should be completed by you and others serving your best clients at the end of *every* engagement.

Client Retention Planning

The intent of client retention planning is to spot situations where you need to take steps quickly and surely to secure the relationship with the client. Client retention planning involves analysis, planning, action, and follow-up. One without the others is insufficient.

> *Analysis* requires an accurate, client-centered description of the situation: "Who is involved in what ways?" "What specifically has been observed/heard/done that suggests dissatisfaction?" "How urgent is it that this situation be handled?"

> *Planning* involves assigning responsibility; allocating resources such as information, budget, and time; and developing a time-phased action program.

> *Action* is the execution of the planned activities.

> *Follow-up* is the act of checking today's reality against the situation defined earlier.

Congratulations! You have completed an important step in the development of your client-centered marketing program. In the next chapter we'll discuss the procedures to be followed in working with your targets of influence.

FIGURE 11–1
Policy and Checklist for Vulnerable Client Situations

In every relationship there is a vulnerability for things to go sour. In a service environment vulnerable situations will always arise when service is substandard. While your organization aims at providing quality service, in certain situations there may still be vulnerability. If the response to any of the following questions is positive, look at the impact it may have. Within the last twelve months:

	Yes	No
1. Have we been late in meeting our commitments?	☐	☐
2. Have we put new personnel on the engagement team?	☐	☐
3. Have we had to replace any of the team members to satisfy the client?	☐	☐
4. Have we given bad advice that has cost the client money?	☐	☐
5. Have we taken key members of the client service team off the account?	☐	☐
6. Have any key members of the client service team left the firm?	☐	☐
7. Have we disagreed with the client on important issues?	☐	☐
8. Has the client appointed a new chief executive?	☐	☐
9. Has a new key board member been appointed?	☐	☐
10. Does the CEO have a close relationship with an individual in another competitive firm?	☐	☐
11. Is the client served by a bank or an attorney who does not respect us?	☐	☐
12. Have we missed regular monthly contact with the client?	☐	☐
13. Have we received limited or no calls for consultation?	☐	☐
14. Is the client in financial trouble?	☐	☐
15. Is there dissatisfaction on the client's part with our industry knowledge?	☐	☐
16. Have we surprised the client lately with a significant issue?	☐	☐
17. Have we reversed a position on advice given previously?	☐	☐
18. Is the personal chemistry between any key member of the client service team and client management a problem?	☐	☐
19. Is there a political situation brewing in the client organization?	☐	☐
20. Do we have limited relationships?	☐	☐
21. Are there effectively no relationships between the partner and client?	☐	☐
22. Does the client have a history of rotating service providers?	☐	☐
23. Has the client acquired a company or business served by another firm that offers similar services?	☐	☐
24. Is the client's parent company served by others who compete with us?	☐	☐
25. Has the client been recently acquired by a company with other service providers?	☐	☐
26. Is the client vulnerable to takeover?	☐	☐

Source: Adapted from Dick Connor, Increasing Revenue from Your Clients (New York: John Wiley & Sons, 1989), p. 203.

CHAPTER 12

Developing Your Targets of Influence

This chapter extends the information about nonclient influentials introduced in Chapter 9. Targets of influence refer to the additional relationships you seek to develop with targeted attorneys, bankers, editors, executive directors of industry associations, community leaders, and others who can provide you with leads or vouch for your ability to serve.

Upon conclusion of this chapter you will be able to:

☐ Identify additional nonclient influentials with whom you want to develop a referral-driven relationship.

☐ Create and maintain favorable visibility with them.

☐ Develop relationships with them based on mutual interest.

☐ Further develop the relationship into a referral-producing relationship.

☐ Develop the know-how to avoid receiving undesirable referrals.

IDENTIFYING ADDITIONAL TARGETS OF INFLUENCE

Your task is to identify the names of additional nonclients who influence and impact your targeted industry-market niches. In addition to the sources listed in Chapter 9, consider these sources:

- Clients who are served by other noncompeting consultants they respect
- Other current nonclient referral sources who are interested in expanding their network of relationships with others they respect
- Announcements of new noncompeting firms who may be future reciprocal referral relationships such as attorneys and accountants

CREATE A FAVORABLE VISIBILITY
WITH TARGETS OF INFLUENCE

Creating an initial and continuing favorable visibility requires planning followed by action. After you develop your list of names, determine where these targets congregate; make it a point to attend the functions they attend; and arrange introductions through mutual friends or sponsors of the events.

One of my public relations clients developed a referral relationship with a highly influential source. My client, during a visit to London, made a cold, drop-in contact telling the target " . . . since we are both in the same field, and I happened to be in town, I thought it made sense to say hello and develop a relationship." Within a year, this London source arranged for my client to make a keynote address to a highly influential group of potential contacts for my client's specialized type of services in London.

In lieu of face-to-face contact, sending a note of congratulations for an award or event in which the possible contact was featured is appropriate. We both receive many contacts from others serving our types of clients after they have read our books. Some of these noncompetitive contacts have developed into good referral sources.

DEVELOP A RELATIONSHIP BASED
ON MUTUAL INTEREST

We've found it useful to take the initiative when developing a long-term relationship with a target. We ask, "Don, does it make sense for us to move into a mutually beneficial referral mode? Serving the . . . niche is one of my current goals, and I'd be glad to think through with you how we can assist each other in using our relationship and reputation in getting leads." At this point we show him a previously prepared preferred prospective client profile. (See Figure 12–1). We review the criteria we have for desirable clients, and also what constitutes my knock-out factors.

What we are really doing is reviewing our criteria for classifying

FIGURE 12–1
Preferred Prospective Client Profile

Positive Characteristics of "A" Client

1. _____
2. _____
3. _____
4. _____
5. _____
6. _____
7. _____
8. _____
9. _____

Knock-Out Factors—"C" and "D" Clients

1. _____
2. _____
3. _____
4. _____
5. _____
6. _____
7. _____

Source: Richard A. Connor, Jr., and Jeffrey P. Davidson, *Getting New Clients* (New York: John Wiley & Sons, 1987), p. 46.

"A" clients (discussed in Chapter 4). Being up-front eliminates a lot of misunderstanding between you and the new source and prevents many potentially expensive problems in serving marginal clients you felt you had to take to keep the relationship alive with the new referral source.

A Word of Warning. Don't move too quickly in your goal of exchanging your Rolodexes with each other. We do this only after we've checked out the ethics, reliability, and staying power of the possible new referral source.

DEVELOPING A REFERRAL-
PRODUCING RELATIONSHIP

A referral-producing relationship simply grows out of the previous steps. One of you provides the other with the name(s) of clients they are comfortable in having you contact or, better still, in arranging for introductions.

Make an Early Decision about the
New Relationship

Give the new relationship a six- to nine-month trial. If the names are flowing and the contacts agree to meet with you, fine. If you experience undue difficulty in getting in to see the leads, once again review your preferred prospective client profile with the source to be certain you are in harmony and can attract desirable new clients.

List the names of targeted contacts under the targets of influence section on your personal marketing plan.

This concludes Part Three. You have developed a new framework for marketing and are now ready to develop a marketing mix that will assist you in capitalizing on the targets you have identified.

PART FOUR

Print-Related Promotion

The marketing and promotional tools of the trade discussed in the next eight chapters directly support a client-centered marketing program serving as complements (and when necessary, alternative vehicles) to personal promotion, which is discussed in Part Five.

A variety of promotional tools is presented in this section, including writing client-centered action letters, writing and using articles, tapping the local press, using direct mail, producing winning proposals, using desktop publishing as a marketing tool, building a brochure, and advertising for results. Where possible, we have eliminated a discussion of costly or time-consuming promotional vehicles that are routinely undertaken by large firms but which often prove to be unfeasible for small- to medium-sized firms.

Recent developments in personal computer technology and desktop publishing, however, enable even the one-person practitioner to execute a variety of affordable marketing techniques. The print-related promotional vehicles you employ should be looked upon as tools to enhance your personal promotion efforts in support of your overall marketing plan. Well-developed print-related promotional materials help set the stage for when you meet with prospective clients and, in some cases, actually prompt others to retain your services.

The order in which we discuss these vehicles does not reflect their importance or potential effectiveness for your firm. Also, depending on the nature of your services, some will be more applicable to you than others. As you read these chapters, list your next period promotion actions in Section 4 of the personal marketing plan (Figure 27–2).

CHAPTER 13

Developing Client-Centered Action Letters

The management action letter is important in the professional-client relationship and often either immediately precedes or follows a personal selling opportunity.

If you are not routinely writing management action letters as part of your overall print-related promotional strategy you want to give special attention to this chapter. A well-composed letter that addresses the needs of a prospective client can be as powerful as any other marketing vehicle. The letter must display the same level of quality as you offer in rendering your professional service.

This chapter provides you with the answers to these questions.

☐ Why are most letters written from the wrong perspective?

☐ How could these statements be changed to reflect a client-centered approach?

"When we examined the Northside Branch we observed that X, Y, Z . . . "

"We feel that our recommendations for an improved reporting system have not been followed."

☐ Are your clients more inclined to take action because your letter suggests action that will provide an acknowledged benefit, or because

they'll be operating in accordance with "generally accepted procedures"?

☐ What type of letter headings are most likely to gain client cooperation?

☐ How can one avoid overemploying the same words in written communications?

PUTTING YOUR LETTERS IN PERSPECTIVE

Most management action letters are written from the perspective of
the professional who develops them. This is because it's easier to write from
one's own perspective.

For example, an account executive with an aggressive advertising
agency in Missouri took an "audit" of his management action letters. He
relates that "I was appalled at the 'I'-centeredness of my letters—"I will send
you . . ." rather than "You will receive . . . ," and so on. "I also found that
I tended to 'push' services we provide rather than suggest solutions to actual
client needs."

A good way to calculate the effectiveness of a management action
letter is to count the number of times "I" or "we" is used rather than "you"
or the equivalent. The following excerpts are from actual letters. The first set
indicate the "I/we" orientation, which should be avoided:

1. "In *our* review, *we* noted the poor control in data processing. . . ."

2. "*Our* personnel had to develop schedules to assist X, Y, Z. . . ."

3. "*We* are pleased to inform you that *our* recommendations made
. . . ."

Here is how each example can be changed to convey the same
meaning with the use of a client-centered approach:

1. "*Management* will want to improve controls in the data processing
area. . . ."

2. "*Management* could realize reduced costs if *internal personnel* are
used to develop schedules which X, Y, Z. . . ."

3. "The *sales staff* is to be complimented for greatly improving. . . ."

You'll find that the client-centered management letter will be more readily
accepted by the client and will enhance your relationship.

USE THE CLIENT'S LANGUAGE

Client-centered management action letters should influence the client to change because of the benefits that will be derived, and not because the client will be operating in accordance with some generally accepted procedure or standard. Here are two excerpts from actual management letters used by professionals in correspondence with clients:

1. "Better standards of documentation should be adopted immediately to conform with the guidelines established in QRS Company's specification manual."

2. "The company does not maintain a fixed asset ledger as is normal procedure for an organization the size of GHI Corporation."

This terminology should be restated, using client-centered terminology so that the benefits of the recommendations being made are clearly spelled out. The preceding passages could be rewritten thus:

1. "Better standards of documentation will assure the company of uninterrupted operations in the event of a sudden turnover in personnel."

2. "The company could benefit in two ways if a fixed asset ledger were developed and maintained: (a) you would reduce the risk of losing valuable assets, and (b) you would be better able to determine the most favorable methods of depreciation for tax purposes."

HEADINGS THAT SUGGEST ACTION

The client-centered management letter can also be used in other ways to win the client's cooperation. Find a letter that you recently sent, and compare the number of headings and subheadings relating directly to your services. The headings might be:

Management Training	Employee Communication
Advertising	Data Collection
Insurance	Payroll
New Products	Inventory
Auditing	Expansion

Now consider varying your headings in a way that would arouse interest. For example:

Upgrading Management Skills	Communicating with Your Staff
Increasing Advertising Effectiveness	Improving Your Management Information System
Maintaining Full Insurance Coverage	Reducing Payroll Costs and Related Expenses
Establishing a Climate for New Innovations	Improving Inventory Control
Preparing for an Audit	Managing Your Expansion

MORE READABLE LETTERS

Here are other suggestions to make your management action letter more readable and useful to the client. Mark weaknesses that are uncorrected items from the previous management letters. Then indicate to the client that the operating efficiency of the company is contingent on its ability to correct these weaknesses. Another technique is to provide space for an "Action Taken" column so that your clients may check off those areas in which corrective measures are taken.

Procedures for Developing Action Letters

If possible, deliver the action letter in person. This helps to build the professional-client relationship and increases the client's propensity to follow the suggestions you have given in the letter.

Here are three ways to determine whether your procedure for developing action letters yields a good-quality letter. First, does the time charged to letter writing frequently overrun original budget estimates or fees that exceed estimates given to clients? Second, are management action letters written and submitted on a timely basis or long after services have been provided (and in the case of a prospective client, long after the initial discussion)? Finally, have guidelines been established to ensure that letters are carefully edited and that the final message is appropriate and on target?

Every letter (including nonmanagement action letters) that you send to a client or target of influence carries "promotional weight." Seek opportunities from the very beginning of your professional relationships to use action letters to best advantage. Later, standard letters can be developed and used for routine events such as greeting new clients, thanking targets of influence for referrals, and reminding clients of deadlines, opportunities, and the like.

Samples of two new business analyses made by an accountant in Denver that led to increased business from existing clients are given in Examples 1 and 2.

Through observation, data collection, and follow-up, the accounting firm influenced a client to purchase additional services:

EXAMPLE 1

Observations: Inventory turnover in the last five years had decreased from nine times a year to four times a year. The company was experiencing an inventory buildup and cash shortage even though sales had increased steadily over the years.

Data Collection: An examination of the available inventory data and inquiry of management revealed the following:

> No substantial improvement in the level of customer service has been achieved by the buildup in inventory.
>
> The company had a problem with obsolescence of inventory (items had been bought in greater quantities than needed to achieve price breaks).
>
> Buying decisions were made without adequate emphasis on inventory management.

Management Letter: Communicated to management the benefits to be achieved from an automated purchasing system integrated with the inventory system.

Result: The accounting firm was engaged to develop and install a system to assist buyers, based on certain inventory management criteria.

EXAMPLE 2

Observations: The client had separate bank accounts for separate operating units. Some accounts had large cash balances, whereas others had overdrafts (suggesting an opportunity for better cash management).

Data Collection: An examination disclosed that there were bank charges on some accounts and cash lying idle in others, and that over a dozen operating units were writing separate checks to the same vendors each month.

Management Letter: Communicated to management the potential benefits of consolidating payables into a single account and using an improved accounts payable automated system. This would (1) pool cash, (2) reduce bank charges, (3) provide better cash management, (4) provide revenue from the excess cash, (5) decrease clerical effort, and (6) organize the payables procedure. (The recommendations emphasized the *benefits* to be achieved rather than the problems diagnosed.)

Result: After receiving a favorable response from the client, the accounting firm proposed an engagement to install an improved, automated accounts payable system utilizing a central bank account and pooled cash funds. This proposal was accepted.

A checklist summarizing the elements of effective client-centered management letters is provided in Figure 13–1.

Using Alternative Words

With action letters, and other forms of written marketing communications, too often, we become fixated toward using particular words and begin unconsciously to develop a mundane, routine style of writing. While this style may be perfectly adequate, overemploying the same words and phrases ultimately weakens your marketing impact and does not contribute to personal development.

Listed below are 100 words commonly employed in business and marketing documents, followed by alternative words for each of the original 100. This list provides a handy mini-thesaurus that can be referred to in the office, at home, or on location.

> *adequate*   satisfactory, sufficient, tolerable, enough
>
> *allocate*   allot, dispose, place, apportion
>
> *also*   additionally, and, too, as well, besides, furthermore, moreover

FIGURE 13–1
Checklist for Effective Client-Centered Management Action Letters

---

☐ Have you reduced the "we" orientation of letters?

☐ Have you complimented clients where possible?

☐ Have you stressed the benefits of implementing recommendations instead of recanting established procedures?

☐ Have you organized management letters by area of client interest instead of by your industry's terminology?

☐ Have you established guidelines that provide realistic estimates of the time required to develop a top-quality letter?

---

analysis breakdown, classification, commentary, differentiation, discussion, inquiry, mathematics, separation, theorization, investigation

analyze break down, classify, differentiate, discriminate, discuss, dissect, reason, explain

any anything, some, every, one

apparent appearing, probable, visible, plain, evident, clear, obvious

apparently externally, seemingly, visibly

approach address, arrive, converge, resemble

approximate near, relative, similar, approaching

approximately nearly, virtually

area location, region, size, space

arrange classify, order, influence, direct, place, group

assist help, aid, subsidize, remedy, support, back

assure affirm, convince, guarantee, make sure, promise, pledge, warrant

basic underlying, simple, essential, vital, main, chief, essential, fundamental

basis cause, foundation, justification, motive, premise

bias deviation, bend, partiality, preference, tendency, influence, prejudice, induration

business activity, affair, commerce, company, duty, occupation, undertaking, vocation, trade

calculate compute, measure, plan, figure, tally, determine

capability ability, preparedness, skill, talent

capital funds, means, resources, cash, money, assets, property, wealth

chance gamble, possibility, opportunity, probability, prospect

check audit, compare, examine, monitor, review, investigate, test

choose desire, select, pick, decide on

collect assemble, procure, compile, store, join, gather, accumulate

company association, firm, group, unit, business

contract agreement, undertaking, promise, pact

control   direct, govern, influence, rule, command

copy (v.)   imitate, duplicate, remake, reproduce

copy (n.)   facsimile, carbon, print

decrease   diminish, reduce, subtract, lessen, decline, dwindle

demonstrate   display, explain, cite, check, prove, represent, show, exhibit

denote   indicate, signify, designate

determine   decide, discover, learn, resolve, settle

discuss   confer, debate, analyze, deliberate, consider

exhibit   display, flaunt, illustrate

fact   truth, evidence, information, certainty, reality

fail   neglect, weaken, fall short, decline, insufficient, miss

finally   consequently, eventually, last, in conclusion

get   acquire, become, discover, incur, obtain, receive, take, secure

go   become, depart, extend, move, operate, progress

guidelines   plans, precepts, rules

have   experience, permit, possess, receive, own, hold

help   aid, facilitate, serve, subsidize, assist, support, back, encourage

inadequate   incomplete, ineffective, insufficient, unsatisfactory

include   combine, comprise, enclose, join, embrace, involve

increase   add to, advance, amplify, develop, multiply, enlarge, extend, prolong

information   data, figures, report, facts, knowledge

item   commodity, component, part, element

labor   occupation, task, work

list   record, inventory, enumeration, register, roll

literature   written matter, writing, lore

location   place, position, site, spot, area

maintain   defend, retain, support, sustain, keep, continue

make   accomplish, acquire, cause, compel, convert, create, execute, perform, manufacture, produce, form, build, construct

manage   direct, govern, control, handle, lead, pilot, operate, supervise, administer *method*   plan, way, system, technique, approach, means

modify   change, diversity, quality, alter, vary, adjust

nation   country, population, community, republic

national   public, universal

normal   average, common, customary, natural, ordinary, typical, healthy, source, whole

number   amount, numeral, sum, total, collection, quantity

objective   intention, will, goal, purpose, commitment, aim

observe   examine, see, watch, notice, witness, regard

obviously   visibly, plainly, clearly, positively, really, certainly, surely, evidently

operate   plot, sum, pilot, act, use, manage

organization   association, unit, business, entity, company, firm, corporation

organize   reorder, arrange, position, unite

original   basic, causal, fundamental, native, new, preceding

perform   accomplish, execute, produce, achieve

points   items, particulars, tips, topics

procure   acquire, induce, purchase, elicit, obtain

produce   accomplish, cause, create, indicate, perform, yield, supply

product   commodity, end product, result, sum, yield, stock

proposal   intention, offer, project, program, scheme

provide   allow, yield, give, supply, furnish, equip

purpose   function, intention, meaning, resolution, object, end, aim

question   issue, puzzle, query, remark, topic, inquiry, interview, ask

rank   classify, judge, align, order, arrange, grade, standing

readily   eagerly, easily, willingly, promptly, quickly

reduce   contract, decrease, denote, depress, diminish, shorten, simplify, subdue, lessen

report   account, record, document, testimony

represent   delineate, describe, mediate, substitute for, act

resolve   analyze, decide, determine, reconcile, solve, conclude, confirm

resource   capital, skill, reserve, source of supply

review   commentary, discussion, examination, narrative, study

scan   discuss, examine, judge, re-examine, study, analyze, browse, skim

shift   convert, change, move, remove, deviate, vacillate

solve   explain, resolve, answer, unravel

source   motive, origin, beginning

study   consider, discuss, examine, seek

system   nature, order, plan, way

take   acquire, entail, receive, believe, pick, choose, select, remove, lift, win, capture, siege

thus   hence, so, similarly, in this way

trend   course, direction, flow, fashion

ultimate   eventual, final, farthest, top, last

use   employ, exploit, deal with, consume, expand

venture   investment, undertaking, speculation

work   function, effort, labor, task, vocation, position

yield   provide, submit, give, relinquish, supply

The use of management action letters expanded to proposals is discussed further in Chapter 17.

CHAPTER 14
Writing and Using Articles

Your firm can enjoy a large number of benefits when you have an article printed in a business or professional publication. There are also, however, some misconceptions about what getting published will do for the firm. Unfortunately, the misconceptions often diminish the positive net benefit that getting published provides because of high author expectations. In this chapter we examine the benefits that getting published does and does not provide. We also discuss using someone else's article to reinforce a point you'd wish to make to a client. The questions to be addressed include:

☐ What are some of the primary benefits of getting published?

☐ What are the secondary benefits of getting published?

☐ What are the best topics for articles?

☐ What are the basic steps in writing an article, starting from scratch?

☐ How can you easily overcome writer's block?

☐ What place does getting an article published have in your overall marketing effort?

☐ How can you get mentioned in the articles others are writing?

PUBLISHING OPPORTUNITIES ABOUND

The number of general, industrial, business, professional, and in-house publications has risen dramatically in the last ten years. By using *Ulrich's International Periodicals Directory, Bacon's Publicity Checker, Working Press of the Nation Writer's Market, Standard Periodicals Directory,* or *Gebbie's All in One Directory,* you can obtain the name, address, telephone number, editorial content, fees paid, circulation, target audience, and submission requirements for over 18,000 journal magazines!

There are also over 12,000 newsletters in the United States today, with thousands more worldwide, and the number is growing at an exponential rate. The *Newsletter Yearbook,* or the *Oxbridge Directory of Newsletters* is particularly useful. Publication within newsletters may yield the same actual benefits as can be achieved through publication in the larger trade magazines. The net benefits for you and your firm, of course, are contingent on the match between the target market of the newsletter and your targets of opportunity and influence. For a magazine or a journal, ask for a sample issue to review, and later write to the editor to relay your article theme.

BENEFITS OF GETTING PUBLISHED

The primary benefits of getting published include the following:

1. Building the firm's reputation
2. Establishing your credentials
3. Creating a favorable impression
4. Bolstering the firm's marketing tools
5. Providing or generating inquiries
6. Being invited to speak to groups

Let's examine each benefit in detail.

Getting published *establishes credentials* for you and your firm in the article topic area. If a partner in an engineering firm, for example, writes an article on reinforcing bridge supports, a public notice has been made that the firm has expertise in this area and may provide assistance in this area. A similar example can be drawn for nearly any topic.

You can *create a favorable impression* by supplying associates with a reprint of an article you have published. Modesty aside, most authors are very proud of their work and have no qualms about submitting reprints to friends, relatives, and associates. Most business associates are pleased and impressed to accept your article reprint. Although they may not say so directly, they may also revel in your small glory and serve as ambassadors for you by informing others.

Many firms maintain in reception areas a notebook that includes the articles and publications of their employees. The articles discuss a wide variety of topics within the fields of specialization. Visitors to the office are impressed by the writing skills and subject expertise of the company staff.

Another benefit of getting published is that the publication or article reprint helps *bolster your firm's brochures and marketing portfolios*. You can include reprints in all your correspondence, including proposals. A high-quality article reprint on glossy stock also increases the effect of a direct mail campaign.

The placement of articles in professional or trade journals may provide or generate *inquiries from potential clients*. After a writer from a local public relations firm has published an article in the Sunday edition of the newspaper (perhaps in the business and finance section or in the style section), some phone calls and inquiries may be generated as a direct result. For magazine publications, readership response to the article is less clearly defined. However, some readers viewing the article may (1) clip or photocopy the article for future reference and (2) contact you for further information, comments, or assistance.

A final benefit is that an article will often result in your *being invited to speak* before a particular group. In actuality, every article can be made into a speech and vice versa. Thus the opportunity to repeat your message locally to defined markets should not be overlooked.

STARTING FROM SCRATCH

Writing an effective, thought-provoking article requires paying close attention to established guidelines plus injecting a healthy dose of individual creativity. If you are attempting your first article, or simply seek a formula to guide you, follow these five steps to craft a publishable article: prewriting, free writing, preparing the first draft, revising, and editing.

Prewriting

This is the stage where an idea or topic is hatched. Your topic may come in a flash or be the result of oscillation between various topics. In any case prewriting requires time. If you attempt to jump into a topic without giving it careful thinking, you're liable to convey to your readers just that—you didn't think very much about the topic.

After exploring possible topics, choose an aspect, an angle, a slice that you can manage. If you're an environmental consultant, for example, rather than writing about the greenhouse effect and its implication, you could focus your article on the experiences of a particular county or town or single family in the Midwest. Then, ask yourself questions about the topic. What are the key issues? What angle has not been explored? How do those affected feel about the situation?

The more questions you can generate, the better. The questions help you to focus your efforts better. During prewriting you will also find it helpful to read and talk about your topic to others, particularly some of your clients. Be a sponge to your topic.

By now a basic question will emerge that enables you to identify a key issue. Ask yourself the question, "What is this like?" For example, if you've decided to write about the effects of the drought on a small farm, "What is this like?" could be "like trying to conduct one's affairs in a sauna." If a phrase or sentence captures the central focus of your topic, use it, explore it, and play with it.

Free Writing

Free writing is plunging in and writing to get your thoughts concerning your basic question thus far onto the page. You may be able to skip free writing if you are able to formulate a thesis, the single sentence that declares "what you will aim to show in your article as a whole." Generally, though, free writing will help you to form your thesis.

By writing rapidly without worrying about organization or content, you can easily generate or capture additional thoughts about your topic and help to establish or refine your thesis statement. A well-chosen thesis statement energizes and focuses your entire article and makes the reader's job easier.

Free writing also aids you in finding your tone. Will you be witty or serious? Conservative or bold? Accusative or nurturing? Whatever you choose, the tone in your thesis statement and the body of the article should match.

Preparing the First Draft

Yes, there will be more than one draft (even if you dictate). First, organize or list the points developed during prewriting and free writing. How will you present them? Chronologically or oppositionally? Or will you opt for cause and effect order, ascending or descending order, or some other method? The choice is yours and is predicated upon your desired impact on the reader.

Next, make an outline of your points, again keeping the reader's interest, education, and possible feelings about the topic in mind. Using the drought example, it is a fair guess that the topic will rouse strong emotions when read by anyone who recently experienced a drought.

Now you are ready to introduce your article with your thesis statement. There are several ways to do this: (1) use a brief lead-up to your statement, (2) employ an anecdote or story that leads to a general thesis, (3) cite a particular case as a generalization that leads to a particular thesis, (4) confront a popular assumption or stereotype, or (5) oppose a particular position.

As you proceed with your article—we recommend dictating the article at this point—use the headings from your outline as guideposts. The headings can even serve as paragraph leads. Think a paragraph at a time. This will make your task easier and ensure a smoother flow. To end your article, either state the implication of your thesis, restate the thesis in terms that broaden its significance, recommend action, answer your initial question, or reaffirm your thesis with a compelling example.

Revising

You must reexamine "the big picture" and carefully refine, tighten, and improve your work. Have you established and maintained a tone? Is the piece slanted toward the niche you wish to reach? Should you reassess or reconsider any of your points? Does your article have unity (all points reinforce your thesis), continuity (flow), and progression (every paragraph offers more information than its predecessor)?

Reread the above section on preparing the first draft. Have you accomplished what you set out to accomplish? Revision can require as much or more work than writing the first draft. This is not time to shortchange your efforts.

Editing

You must make every sentence vital, focused, balanced, and economical. Vary sentence lengths. Check spelling, grammar, and punctuation. Use active verbs. Remember your readers have work to do; help them all you can. Check each sentence carefully—if useful, read them aloud. Tie up all loose ends. Eliminate jargon and unclear words. Trim the fat; if a word or phrase can be eliminated, it probably should be.

After extensive editing, read your article again. Catch any last glitches. Make sure that your final copy adheres to established rules of grammar and style. If so, it is ready to submit for consideration.

SELECTING ARTICLE TOPICS

The best topics for articles are derived from the successful *work that you have already done*. This may include reports, papers, summaries, guides, exhibits, and so on that you previously presented to a client, which can be generalized and applied to a larger audience. You may wish to write an article *with* a client for whom you have produced exceptional results.

Other good topics for articles include those topics that can be addressed by you or any members of the staff. If you're an architect, you may have an excellent article on "tips for success when designing skywalks" in your mind, even though you may never have written about the topic. *Any topic* that can readily be addressed by you or your staff and is of interest to your selected market is a good topic.

If you are developing your credentials in a specific market or functional area, then, by all means, a topic in that specified market or area on which you can write intelligently is an excellent choice. An article that stresses benefits to your clients as a result of working with you is particularly useful.

GENERATING ARTICLE TOPICS

Here are some ways to generate article topics and enable you to get started on the high road to getting published:

1. Make a list of gripes or discomforts in connection with your profession. Regardless of where you work or what you do, a list of gripes can readily be created. Within each gripe lies the seed of a subject for an article. If something bothers you, it undoubtedly bothers others in your field. Discuss the problem in broad industry terms and offer suggestions for redress. The authors have done this on several occasions on the topics of management, marketing, and starting new ventures. By recognizing the universality of a problem that you face in your profession, you will instantly be creating material for an excellent article.

2. Start a clip file of articles that interest you. Every time you read the Sunday newspaper or a professional journal, save those articles that strike your fancy. File all the clippings by topic or subject area. Months later, review your clip file, and to your amazement you will see that what you've clipped serves as the catalyst for numerous article ideas. Freelance writers have successfully used the clip file technique for years.

3. Develop a list of six or eight ways to do something better. The market for "how-to" articles is increasing steadily as more and more clients thirst for "do-it-yourself" information. By introducing a number into the title of the article, such as "Eight Ways to Accomplish XYZ," you have established a hook that will appeal to your selected target market. Take some time right now or after finishing this chapter to draw up some lists of ways to do something better. The number can be assigned when you run out of ways; "Eight Ways to Do Something

Better" could be changed to "Six Ways to Do Something Better" if you can't come up with the additional two. You'll still have an interesting article and one that will be published.

4. Recall your favorite professional experience, biggest disappointment, or other memorable event. If you've been practicing for more than a year, undoubtedly you will have a number of interesting experiences, and these make good starting points for articles.

5. Shorten or adapt larger articles, reports, or papers that you've already done. The fastest way to write an article is to not write—to glean the essence of previous work, update it, improve it, or prepare it from a different perspective. We've gone back through old consulting reports and quickly found two that could be readily converted to publishable articles.

6. Take a contrary view to a popular opinion or method for accomplishing something. With great care and sound reasoning, gently, but convincingly explain why your view or approach is superior or more effective.

Here's a checklist of additional ideas for generating article topics:

☐ Interview a prominent person in your industry.

☐ Make a list of new developments in your profession.

☐ Discuss new legislation, regulation, or other "official" changes in an industry and how it (they) will impact the reader.

OVERCOMING WRITER'S BLOCK

Many professionals who want to write an article never do so for a variety of reasons. If writer's block is a problem, and you can't assign the task to a staff member or can't afford to hire an outside writer, the following suggestions may help you get started:

1. Create a one-page outline of an article idea. Over the years, we've found that producing a one-page outline or as little as ten key words on a page was more than sufficient as guidance through the preparation and completion of an article. The technique of using an outline or one-page list works well because only a 5- to 10-minute time investment is required. Later, when you have time available to write the article, you will find that the outline keeps you on track and hastens efficient manuscript completion.

2. Think about how the phrase "published author" will look on your brochure. By visualizing the rewards of writing and getting your article published, you can break out of the chains that may currently restrain you and get started on an article that you can finish *today*.

3. Avoid extraneous reading. Think of all the times that you read the newspaper and within three days totally forgot 95 percent of what you read. Analyze what the continual reading of the paper has done for your income, career, and life in general, and you might agree, at least somewhat, that you could skip reading the paper now and then, write more articles, and enjoy the benefits of getting published.

4. Clear your desk of everything except what you need to write your article. Recognize that during the time you're preparing an article you must tune out distractions. An effective way to do this is to work on a clear surface.

5. Identify in advance the target audience that will be interested in reading your article. Who will be reading your article and what impact will it have on them? Think of the last time you wrote a letter to a friend or relative and how the words and ideas flowed. Your writing task was on a one-to-one basis, and your target audience was perfectly defined. You can achieve the same effect when you precisely define the target group that will be reading your article. If it's helpful to you, you might write the names of your target group on the top of your outline (e.g., "Peers," "Associations," "Executives Earning Over $80,000 Per Year").

6. Sit down, place your watch in front of you, and start writing for a timed five minutes. Often you will find that you don't wish to stop after five minutes. Getting started is the key obstacle to writing productively. If you can master the "five-minute technique," you will develop a habit that will blast the term "writer's block" out of your vocabulary.

DICTATING: THE END OF WRITER'S BLOCK

An effective way to conquer writer's block is by using the portable dictation equipment that has long been available with countless features at a wide variety of prices. The vast majority of professionals still write out articles in longhand, type them onto a disk, or dictate them to a secretary who transcribes from shorthand. These three methods are prone to writer's block, and furthermore are grossly inefficient for the purposes of writing articles and optimizing the use of time.

When it comes to typing or writing longhand versus the using of portable dictation equipment, the difference is like walking or driving a car in order to reach a destination. Once you become familiar with the ease of operation, the convenience and the pure joy of finishing articles in approximately one-third of the time it used to take you, you'll never again let yourself be without portable dictation equipment. You will probably start taking it with you on trips and after hours to record notes and ideas, to finish letters immediately after meetings, and to get to all the articles that you have wanted to write, but never found the time to do so.

The reason why most professionals haven't converted to portable dictation equipment, based on industry surveys, is that they feel a strong need to see what they are working on. A visual review is indeed helpful; however, this is not a reason to avoid portable dictation equipment. Two factors should be considered:

1. To properly use portable dictation equipment, you must first prepare a good outline of the material to be dictated, the same as if you were initiating a handwritten article. With the outline, key words can be expanded to sentences and paragraphs through dictation. The pause feature on all portable dictation equipment allows you to start and stop at any time to gather thoughts and to articulate complete sentences and paragraphs.

    The sentence just completed required three pauses while dictating; however, as the secretary transcribed the material directly from the tape, there were no unusually long breaks in any sentences (other than those created through use of the foot pedal that controls the speed).

    Portable dictation machines have recall and playback features that allow you to monitor your recording as it progresses. With a good outline, however, your need to review what has been dictated diminishes directly proportional with use of the equipment. The start-up time to become familiar and then proficient with the equipment should average no more than an hour.

2. The need for visual review is overestimated. As you are writing longhand or typing onto a disk, there is a strong need for visual review because you are progressing so slowly. When you are dictating, your mind is working much more rapidly than you can write or even type. As you dictate passages and paragraphs in thirty to forty seconds that formerly required much more time, the need for visual review diminishes markedly.

    The number one reason why professionals say they won't or can't use portable dictation equipment is unfounded. Using portable dictation equipment is directly related to how organized you are personally. If you are able to file material and extract files readily, and if your desk is well organized and your shelves are relatively neat, the chances are that you'll be good at dictating with portable equipment.

The simplest portable recorder and microcassette tape allow for 120 minutes of taping—60 minutes per side. It's a good idea to put each tape in a small envelope along with a label or brief explanation. If you have computations, charts, or other exhibits, merely say "Inclusion No. 1" while taping, and then include the handwritten information on pages that also go in the envelope. Many users merely request that the transcriber skip a specified number of spaces or inches, and then provide the information after receiving the typist's draft.

Every professional service provider who writes more than four hours per week, should use portable dictation equipment. Prices for good equipment start at approximately $300 for the hand-held portable unit and the secretary's transcriber unit.

Here's a checklist for overcoming writer's block:

☐ Create a one-page outline of an article idea.

☐ Think about how the phrase "published author" will look on your brochure.

☐ Avoid extraneous reading; instead, write your article.

☐ Clear your desk of everything except what's needed to write your article.

☐ Identify in advance the target audience that will be reading your article.

☐ Try writing for five minutes and see what happens.

☐ *Speak* instead of writing; use portable dictation equipment.

Most professionals find that once they get started, writing an article is not a difficult task.

AN ALTERNATIVE: INFORMATION BOOKLETS

A useful alternative to writing articles is to publish and distribute an information booklet. A possible title could be: "Facts on Closely Held Corporations," "Tips on Stretching Advertising Budgets," or other literature of general interest to your targets. In no way does this have to be a comprehensive dissertation. However, your targets realize that it is best to hire competent professionals. Thus you can distribute a small information booklet that will be read and will prompt people and firms to contact you. Management consultants, lawyers, and engineers have all successfully distributed "facts-on" booklets.

USE SOMEONE ELSE'S ARTICLE

Finally, consider using an article written by someone else (in which you're not mentioned). If you wish to make an important point to a client, use data, quotes, or studies that support your proposal or service suggestion. For instance, a consultant obtained permission to duplicate an article that summarized the eight key factors found in successful organizations by Peters and Waterman. The consultant sent an accompanying letter to prospects that said, "I disagree with two of the factors discussed in the article and have discovered another factor not identified by the authors. I'll call you next week to see if you would like to discuss your situation and receive a brief description of the 'ninth factor.' "

Getting articles published will serve to supplement a good marketing program but will not, by any means, replace it. Also, the *positive effects of getting an article published are largely temporary*. For six or nine months, you may benefit by being published, but in this age of information and information overload, an article dated March 1992 has less and less impact as 1993 draws near. In combination with the effective use of other marketing tools, a published article can provide useful benefits, indeed.

CHAPTER 15

Tapping the Local Press

An effective method of marketing and promoting a professional practice is through the use of publicity and the local press. Effective publicity and public relations can contribute to your overall marketing effort at little or no cost and in many cases can be more effective than paid advertising and the publicity that paid advertising may "buy."

Fortunately for the small practitioner, the generation of publicity does not require substantial time or effort. What is required is familiarity with techniques designed to generate publicity and implementation of those techniques with which you feel comfortable.

In this chapter you'll gain answers to the following questions:

☐ What is publicity?

☐ What is a news release?

☐ Who can submit news releases?

☐ What are good topics for news releases?

☐ What are some other techniques for using the local press?

PUBLICIZE, PUBLICIZE

For many professionals a sustained advertising campaign is beyond the resources of the firm. Through an effective public relations campaign and the generation of publicity, however, it is possible to use media sources, particularly the local press, to keep your name in front of targets of opportunity.

Public relations involves all planned activities undertaken to influence public opinion. Publicity is a key component of public relations and has been defined as media coverage of events, including background information, descriptions, relevant data, or other current information involving an individual, product (or service), business, or organization.

Contemporary society is media "oriented." Thus one article *about you* in the local paper can generate more publicity, for example, than an expensive, exhaustive direct mail campaign.

YOUR IMAGE ON PAPER

What image are you projecting in your company literature? Are you a local firm? Is your company better established than most of the competition? Do you provide more dependable service? Is your staff better trained and equipped "to serve the client?" Have you been in business longer than the competition? Your firm's image should reflect something unique about your firm, something that makes you stand out from the competition.

For the smaller service firm, but really for any size firm, the image that you project initially often is based on "paper." Many of your prospective clients will make an evaluation of your company based on what they read about you, such as your project literature or your brochure. In cognizance of this reality, becoming the subject of a feature article is a strategic marketing vehicle for enhancing your print image.

Pick up one of your area's business magazines or even the business section of your daily newspaper. Every issue of these publications carries an interview with or feature on a local entrepreneur. The majority of these stories are placed by public relations firms who have been paid by the person the story is about. The profiles you come across are part of a coordinated effort undertaken and funded by the firms or individuals publicized.

Suppose you're an architect in Kansas City, and the city council has voted to raze an historic building. One well-placed interview on the benefits to the community of preserving the structure in its original location is likely to catch the eye of hundreds of developers, city and regional planners, preservation groups, historical societies, and anyone else concerned with architecture and historic preservation.

A Yorkshire, England, cosmetic surgeon wanted to increase his visibility in the community and attract new patients. To highlight and promote his services, he announced he would undergo a face lift to demonstrate his commitment and belief in the service he was providing. He had "before" and "after" photos taken. A public relations agent was hired from the outset to ensure maximum exposure. Within a few weeks following the operation, a major story about the surgeon appeared in one of the region's most prestigious monthly magazines, under the byline of the publicity agent.

To the average Englishman, it would have appeared that the publication either contracted with the writer to produce this story or took the piece "over the transom." Because publishers have known for a long time of the healthy numbers of people in their community who wish to be written about and have the funds to commission an article, the publishers very often get their material for free.

The way in which the services of the architect or surgeon are publicized do not appear as advertisements, but as articles of social or community interest. And, an article about someone is far more influential than an ad taken out by that same person.

It's not always more costly and difficult to get an article written and placed than to simply take out an ad. The cost of getting an article written, which may span several pages and include photos is likely to cost far less than a single page ad in the same publication. While the advance planning, coordination, and acceptance of the self-generated article require considerable effort, it is a very sound investment. A well-placed article in a widely read publication can have a greater impact than an entire year's worth of advertisements (covered in Chapter 20).

NEWS RELEASES TO MEDIA

There are, of course, far less expensive ways to gain publicity. You can submit a news release—that is, information about your firm—to newspapers and radio at no cost and obtain free publicity. Some of the items that make good press releases include promotions of individuals within the firm, the hiring of new personnel, where you will be speaking, contract awards received, relocation or renovation of your offices, results of surveys you've completed, and expansion of your services. Each of these items is sufficient information to make a good news release. A more comprehensive list of news release topics is presented in Figure 15–1.

Read your local newspaper today and you likely will spot two or three news releases about professionals in your area. The releases will state the names of the firm, the locations, what they do, and probably quotes from the principals.

All that is required to have that information in the newspaper is to type up a short, one- or two-page sheet and submit it to the city editor with details regarding whom to contact if follow-up information is desired. Sending a good photograph never hurts. (But don't expect its return!) Remember, there is no "roving reporter." To get a news release published, *you* must develop and send it! A sample is provided in Figure 15–2.

FIGURE 15–1
Good Topics for News Releases

Services
New clients
Studies you've completed
Office expansion, renovation, relocation
New service introduction
New uses for existing products
Lower cost due to more efficient operation
Services that address newsworthy topics
Unusual service offerings
Bids or awards
New contracts

Firm
Affiliations
Equipment installations
Accomplishments
Mergers, acquisitions
Anniversaries of firm, principals, or long-term employees
Association memberships
New building or radical change in office layout
Banquets or awards dinners
Employee training programs
Projected plans
Joint programs—government industry

Promotion
Special distinction
Contests, new offers, premiums
Exhibits, trade show, display
Promotion success story
Visits by notable individuals
Overcoming competitors
New design, trademark, logo
New market areas—industry, geography

Employees
Speaking engagements
Reprints of speeches
Travel abroad
Interesting backgrounds, hobbies
Noteworthy accomplishments
Increase in employee benefits
Employee awards
Retirements, births, deaths
Civic activities
Courses completed, certificates, citations, degrees, licenses
Seminars attended
Software developed
Publications—books, articles
Cassettes, videos produced

Community Activity
Fund-raising events
Program sponsorship, i.e., scholarships to foreign exchange, internships
Memorial, dedication or testimonial ceremonies
Training community labor force
Local news that relates to company
Community exhibits in which company has taken part
Local election to office of company official
Meeting announcements

Research
Survey results
New discoveries
Trends, projections, forecasts
New equipment or facility development

FIGURE 15–2
Sample News Release

George Franks and Company
West Haven Professional Building
Pasadena, California 99999
(818) 888-8888

FOR IMMEDIATE RELEASE
Contact: Sue Powell
888-8888

PASADENA ARCHITECT EXPANDS OFFICE

George Franks and Company, an architectural firm practicing in the Pasadena area for the past four years, recently moved its office to the West Haven Professional Building located near the courthouse downtown.

"This new office," said George Franks, "will enable us to increase both our staff and the range of services provided." In addition, the location is easily accessible by public transportation.

Franks, who first began his practice in Pasadena on King Street in 1980 with a staff of two, now employs a staff of 12, including four junior partners and a full-time editor/production coordinator. The new office, located on the second floor of the Professional Building, occupies 3,600 square feet.

"In the last year and a half it became apparent that our old office had simply become too small and that we could not provide the level of service our clients were accustomed to," Franks said. Franks is a member of the California State Society of Architects and the American Institute of Architecture.

NEWS RELEASE FOLLOW-UP

After submitting your news release, you should undertake the following activities:

News Release Follow-up

It's no typographical error; after you submit a news release to an editor, do nothing. If your release is run, you'll know soon enough. Your associates, friends, and relatives will be calling! However, it is *not* wise or recommended that you:

Call the editor.	Leave messages for the editor.
Ask for clippings.	Visit the editor.
Seek a publication date.	Do anything but wait.

Your release, if used, is printed based on the newspaper's needs, availability of space, prominence of you and your firm, and a host of other factors already at play. Any contact that you attempt to make after submitting a release is usually perceived as an irritation to the editor. "So write'm, send'm, and relax!"

PUBLIC "THANK YOU" MESSAGES

Another way to generate publicity is through a public "thank you" message. This method has been used successfully many times. It is not perceived as an advertisement (although you must pay for it similarly to paid advertising). The objective is to draw attention to your firm by showing appreciation for your clients.

The way to do this is to place an ad, usually to the local news or business section of the newspaper, stating that your firm "wishes to thank its 100 (or the appropriate number) clients for letting us help you with your hopes and dreams. May your coming years be as profitable as the ones that have passed." Variations of this message will also be effective. You then list the name, address, and telephone number of your firm. This message has been known to bring in many calls, and because it does not appear to be advertising, you maintain a low-key, professional image. A sample is presented in Figure 15–3.

OTHER STRATEGIES

Other publicity generators may be effective, depending on your situation:

- *Offer free meeting room.* If you have the room within your offices, you may consider offering free meeting space to local civic organiza-

FIGURE 15–3
Sample Public Thank You Notice

Ronald DeVries and Company
Consulting Engineers
Brussels

Wishes its 150 clients a very
Merry Christmas. Thanks
for sharing your
dreams with us.
May next year
be your best.

---

tions or charities. Such groups may require space for as little as a
few hours one night a month. This is an excellent way to build a
good community image and generate publicity about your firm. The
local press may make mention.

- *Run for public office.* Much publicity and community recognition
  can be gained by running for a noncontroversial public office.
  Granted, funds will have to be spent to develop and distribute campaign literature, but win or lose, you stand to gain broad exposure
  within the community. Although it may appear time-consuming to
  seek public office, it's a fast way to achieve community recognition.

- *Offer a community "good citizen" award.* Each week or month,
  have someone on your clerical staff scan local newspapers and publications to find stories on individuals who have performed some good
  deed for the community. As you select each week's or month's
  winner, send an award or certificate to the individual with a letter
  explaining your program. Duplicate letters should then be sent to
  local media who may wish to report on your award system. If space
  allows, display the names of winners within your office. This will
  draw interest among people who see it. In the long run, maintenance
  of this award system will generate very effective community relations
  and publicity.

LETTERS TO THE EDITOR

Have you ever considered sending a letter to the editor? As a business
professional you certainly have something of merit to say regarding issues
that affect your community. Why not say it on the editorial page?

A published letter to the editor of your local newspaper will be more
effective for marketing purposes than a published letter to the editor in one
of your professional journals. However, even a published letter to the editor
in one of your professional journals can be used for marketing purposes when
an attractive reprint of the letter, including the date, page, and logo of the
publication in which it is contained, is included with your correspondence to
clients and prospects (much as you would use an article). In fact, a well-
written letter to the editor, regardless of the publication in which it appears,
in many instances can serve as an adequate substitute to writing a full-blown
article.

The letter to the editor registers a distinct impact with those who read
it. It positions you as a responsible, authoritative professional who is taking
a leadership and advocacy position on what is presumably an important,
current topic.

FIGURE 15-4
Submitting Letters to the Editor

Type your letter, keeping it short and to the point.

Include your name, affiliation, address, and all telephone numbers (the editor may call you to verify that it was in fact you who sent the letter, or to obtain clarification).

Provide the editor with a title or prelude to your letter, i.e., "In Response to Your Article on XYZ . . ." or "On the Issue of UVW . . ."

Avoid accusative, rhetorical, or cynical overtones.

Suggest a solution, if possible, to the issue or problem to which you have alluded.

The reading public, which may include many of the people you wish to serve, often finds it easier and more interesting to read letters to the editor than articles appearing in the same publication. Because of the single-column, unintimidating appearance of such letters, many people do not hesitate to read one after another.

The key to getting a letter to the editor published in your local newspaper—other than submitting an excellent letter—is speed. Call up the publication in question, inform them that you have a letter to the editor that you would like to send by FAX, and obtain their FAX number. The editor in charge of the letter page will appreciate the quick response and, now and then, will even call you back within 24 hours. Generally, however, your local newspaper receives all the letters it can handle and must select a few from a wide field. So don't be disappointed if yours is not chosen.

Whereas the competition to get into your local paper may be significant, professional, trade, and industry magazines and journals often go begging when it comes to obtaining poignant, thought-provoking letters. As with other articles and news releases, send your letters to more than one publication. If your local newspaper and a professional journal both want to print the letter, you will have no problem. If two professional journals wish to print the same letter, then you must withdraw your letter from one of the publications.

Some guidelines for submitting letters to the editor are presented in Figure 15-4.

Your local press needs you as much as you need them. The successful professional actively uses the press to promote his or her firm.

CHAPTER 16

Using Direct Mail

Direct mail is a unique form of promotion because the letter or message that you enclose can be personalized and distributed to targets of opportunity. Direct mail is flexible in that you can control the timing and scope of the effort. However, the preparation of effective direct mail correspondence often requires the assistance of other professionals. In this chapter we discuss ways direct mail can be used and sources available to you. Specifically, you'll be able to answer the following questions:

☐ What are some of the benefits of using direct mail?

☐ What are the contents, copy style, and format of winning direct mail letters?

☐ What are the five basic components of the overall package?

☐ In what ways can lists be subdivided and precisely targeted to suit your needs?

☐ What is the cost range for a 1,000-name mailing list?

☐ What are three local sources that can be used to develop a mailing list?

THE COVER LETTER—THE FIRST OF FIVE PARTS TO THE DIRECT MAIL PACKAGE

A typical direct mail package contains five elements including the letter, an enclosure, reply slip, reply envelope, and outside envelope. The letter, not coterminous with a client-centered action letter, can readily grab the interest of the prospect, and if properly written, hold his interest all the way through.

Many successful direct mailers follow a standard formula that consists of a four-paragraph letter. The first sentence of the first paragraph sums up the entire letter. The balance of the paragraph introduces what you are announcing. The second paragraph stresses the urgency of your message. Many professionals continue with a sentence about other satisfied clients in the prospect's industry area. Mention something about yourself and about your firm in the third paragraph, and conclude in the fourth paragraph by asking the prospect to take action. This frequently involves asking the prospect to fill out a reply card or to call for more information.

As we recommended in our book, *Getting New Clients,* the most effective message in the close of a client-centered letter is simply to inform the recipient that you will be calling in a few days "to see if it makes sense for us to arrange an appointment."

Many direct mail consultants advise putting a "P.S." after your closing signature. The postscript either reinforces the notion of the prospect taking action or poses a question that he feels compelled to answer, such as, "If you feel that you are not getting your money's worth out of your tax adviser, wouldn't you like to begin spending your money more judiciously?" Note: Depending on what type of service you provide and the type of prospect to whom you are appealing, you may wish to forego the P.S. portion of the letter.

PRODUCING DIRECT MAIL LETTERS THAT GET ACTION

James A. McClain, Vice President of the Sheridan Group based in Washington, DC, advises that before you start to write copy, you should make sure that your suggestions are presented in a manner that outlines their validity and importance to the prospect. Just saying you can help is not enough. There must be an overriding reason for following through on your letter over the other printed information your prospects receive. Figure 16–1 lists McClain's 20 tips, arranged in three categories, for producing high-powered direct mail letters.

FIGURE 16–1
Twenty Tips for Writing Direct Mail Letters That Your Prospects Will Respond To

Strategy and Contents

1. Remember that *people respond to other people.*
2. People prefer dealing with individuals to organizations, so *focus on the prospect, not his organization.*
3. *Get right to the main point and don't digress.* Don't bore your prospects and waste their time with warm-up copy.
4. Make your suggestions *specific and actionable.*
5. *Be realistic about what can be accomplished.*
6. *Avoid asking questions* that may elicit a negative response, such as "Why don't we get started?"
7. *Prospects need direction.* Your ability to provide it will pique their interest.

Copy Style

1. Be *informal* yet professional in your approach, but don't write institutional copy.
2. Put description and narrative into your copy to make the copy flow, but *be concise.*
3. Read the letter aloud to *check the rhythm.*
4. Stay within the bounds of *believability.* Don't exaggerate or scream the message.
5. *Write in clear, simple sentences,* yet be moving and memorable. Remember that anything that can be misunderstood will be misunderstood.
6. *Check for repetition* in words and phrases and replace them whenever appropriate.
7. After completing the copy, ask yourself if the letter is one that *you would like to receive.*

Format

1. Make your letter look like a *personal letter* regardless of the production process.
2. Incorporate *one idea only into each paragraph,* not many.
3. Use *short paragraphs,* not long ones.
4. People seldom read an entire letter, so *underline, indent* and *create different size paragraphs* to hold interest.
5. *There is no ideal length.* Eliminate what is not needed, but state your case thoroughly.
6. Before going to press, *proof the text again and again for accuracy (content, grammar, and format)*—and have two colleagues do the same.

THE DIRECT MAIL PACKAGE

Your *overall package concept is important*. It must work as a unit. Here are some of McClain's suggestions on the four basic contents of the direct mail package, which includes enclosures, reply slip, reply envelope, and outside envelope.

Enclosures

1. An enclosure is used to increase response by providing information that cannot be included in the letter, such as the service offered by your firm and specifics about the project you're discussing. Otherwise, they are not necessary and can decrease the response rate.

2. *Photographs* or graphics can be very effective. They can augment your case for support and increase the response rate.

3. *Newspaper stories* and *endorsement letters* are also good enclosures.

Reply Slip

1. The reply slip should be a *self-contained easy-to-follow document*.

2. *Keep the reply slip simple* to read and to complete.

3. *Include a return address* in case, for whatever reason, a prospect does not have a reply envelope.

4. Print the reply slip on colored paper stock so that it stands out from the rest of the package.

Reply Envelope

1. Windowed reply envelopes are good to use in direct mail pieces that have prospect information labels on the reply slip (with the return address on the back). This ensures that the prospect identification information will be returned and that the mail is returned to your institution.

2. Include your firm's *motto or credo* on the envelope.

3. Use *first class* stamps for prospects.

4. Have the envelope addressed *to an individual and address the reply envelopes*.

Outside Envelope

1. Mail *first class* rather than bulk to top prospects.

2. *Use commemorative stamps,* when appropriate, not metered or indicia'd envelopes.

3. *Type the names and addresses* rather than use a label.

4. *Use envelopes that are not the standard* #10 size. (The 6″ x 9″ size, which looks like an invitation, is effective.)

5. Do not use self-mailers.

Avoid using bulk rate postage and computer-generated labels. While it is easier and cheaper to use them, it does not help to convey a high-quality image and certainly does not indicate that you have specifically targeted this prospect for a needed service.

Always, always, always address your direct mail piece to a specific individual or, if that information is not available, a specific known title within the company or organization. Otherwise, it is all but guaranteed that your direct mail piece will be tossed.

THE MAILING CYCLE

Many firms have successfully used direct mail and are in the habit of making specialized mailings throughout the year (see Figure 16–2). For example, the distribution of professional holiday greeting cards is a standard in many industries and represents a simple form of direct mail.

Using Direct Mail

Some firms purchase lists or use in-house developed lists for a special mailing to coincide with the year's end and start of the new year. Such mailings emphasize the firm's ability to provide assistance in the year ahead.

Larger firms have found that the compilation of mailing lists is a key element in the development and growth of the practice. For targeted industries in which you have particularly strong experience, you may decide to experiment with the use of mailing lists to see what your returns are. If you have strong experience with advertising agencies, for example, you could order a mailing list through a list compiler that provided the names of thousands of advertising agencies across the country.

FIGURE 16–2
Monthly Mailing Themes

Month	Theme(s)
Month	*Theme(s)*
January	New Year's
	End of tax year
	Martin Luther King Day
	Inventory reduction
February	Presidential sales
March	Getting ready for spring
April	Income tax returns
	Increase daylight hours
	Spring cleaning
May	May Day
	Start of tourist season
June	Graduations
July	U.S. Independence Day
	Bastille Day (France)
August	Dog days of summer
September	Labor Day
	Jewish New Year
	Back to school
	Recharge efforts
October	Beginning of government fiscal year
	Octoberfest (Germany)
November	Harvest
	U.S. Thanksgiving
December	Holidays
	Reduce inventory
	Time off

FOCUSING IN ON YOUR TARGETS

If you wish to focus more narrowly on your state, region, or metropolitan area, you're in luck, because major list compilers offer this capability. Any competitive list house can offer these types of special selections.

State selection	Net worth
City metro area selection	Financial rating
Test cross sections	SIC code
Title addressing	Occupational title selection
Number of employees	Other special selections
Sales volume	Related services

Within the area of advertising agencies, one New York-based list house maintains a list of 19,000 advertising agencies and counselors, 27,000 advertising agency executives, 3,600 major advertising agencies, and 3,000 advertising agency presidents.

The cost of a mailing list generally ranges from $50 to $120 per 1,000 names. Virtually all mailing list compilers rent their list for one-time use only, unless otherwise stated. Many provide outright sales of the mailing list for unlimited use within a designated period of time—often one year. Under this arrangement the cost of the list is understandably much more expensive than for one-time use.

INFORMATION SOURCES

Scores of list compilers offer selected names within any industry, on demand. For example, *The List House* (800) 634–1949 supplies data on businesses and consumers in five formats including mailing labels, 3×5 cards, magnetic tapes, PC diskettes, and prospect lists, and provides an array of available data: 16 million businesses in the United States, 3.4 million businesses in Canada, 526,000 physicians and dentists, 423,000 lawyers, and so forth.

Within consumer markets, the service offers breakouts of 4.3 million high-income Americans, 79 million households, 9 million high school and college students, 300,000 new home owners, and other types of lists. These lists can be broken down further by region, state, country, town, ZIP code, section of city, and neighborhood.

If you're interested in pursuing direct mail as a marketing vehicle for your firm, the following additional sources of information will be useful:

> Alvin B. Zeller, Inc.
> 224 Fifth Avenue (6th Floor)
> New York, New York 10001
> (212) 689–4900
> (800) 223–0814 out of state

This supplier offers lists by state, county, city, metro area, ZIP code and/or SIC on label, magnetic tape, floppy disk, or 3×5 card.

> American Business List, Inc.
> P.O. Box 27347
> Omaha, Nebraska 68127
> (402) 331–7169

American Business List, Inc. compiles and frequently updates large-scale prospect lists from the Yellow Pages.

Hugo-Dunhill Mailing List, Inc.
630 Third Avenue
New York, New York 10017
(212) 682–8030
(800) 223–6454 out of state

Also:

(404) 885–1490—Atlanta
(312) 726–2177—Chicago
(213) 469–8231—Los Angeles
(202) 783–5988—Washington, DC

Hugo-Dunhill offers comprehensive mailing lists and related services, and multiple formats.

Research Project Corporation
4 South Pomperaug Avenue, Box 449
Woodbury, Connecticut 06798
(203) 263–0100
(800) 243–4360

Direct Marketing Association
6 East 43rd Street
New York, New York 10017
(212) 689–4977

The Direct Marketing Association provides support, information, and guidance in the application of effective direct marketing techniques.

International Business Lists, Inc.
162 North Franklin Street
Chicago, Illinois 60606
(312) 236–0350
(800) 535–0350

International Business Lists, in business for over 30 years, specializes in the compilation of business, professional, and institutional lists representing a data base of over 10 million names.

R.L. Polk and Company
6400 Monroe Boulevard
Taylor, Michigan 48180
(313) 292–3200

R.L. Polk offers most of what the other list houses offer, as well as comprehensive consumer lists by alphabet, phone number, and street address for specific geographic markets. The information is available on labels, 3×5 cards, magnetic tape, and in loose-leaf manuscript. Now in its 120th year, Polk has branch offices in 15 major cities.

Contacting Direct-Mail Consultants

The managing partner of a firm that had made no use of direct mail decided to investigate the use of the tool. He asked several of his clients for the names of their direct mail consultants and talked with others to obtain ideas and names of possible suppliers. He asked the suppliers what direct experience they had in creating direct mail campaigns for similar firms.

For suppliers who passed the first hurdle, he then asked: "How much time do you estimate that it would take you to learn specifically about us and develop a central theme and cost-effective campaign for building name recognition and stimulating inquiries?"

Only the firms that pointed out the futility of such a campaign were asked to submit a proposal for building a continuing direct mail campaign for the firm to accomplish the primary goal of taking the "chill" out of the initial telephone contact.

DEVELOPING YOUR OWN LISTS

There are numerous other sources from which target lists can be generated:

1. Your local Yellow Pages directory
2. The roster of members of the local Chamber of Commerce
3. Attendees at trade shows
4. Newspaper advertisers
5. Blue and red books or other commercial directories

The cost of compiling these lists, developing targeted letters and other information, and mailing should be weighed against the potential for developing new business. Traditionally direct mail campaigns generate a 1 to 2 percent return, although this return can be greatly exceeded if bolstered by follow-up telephone calls, additional mailings, and adherence to the client-centered, leveraging, marketing approach.

CHAPTER 17

Producing Winning Proposals

An increasing number of clients and prospective clients are asking professional service firms to prepare proposals as a prerequisite to initiating an engagement. A proposal can be viewed as a logical extension of a management action letter.

The key to writing a successful proposal is to obtain current information on the nature, scope, and needs of the target or a particular solicitation and to present information within the proposal in a manner that convinces the target that hiring your firm represents the best way to accomplish the task. Yet, writing a superior proposal will never substitute for effective personal selling. This necessarily large chapter will enable you to answer these questions:

☐ What is a proposal?

☐ What are the sections contained in an effective proposal?

☐ How does the client-centered proposal process work?

☐ What is a concept paper? How does it enhance your marketing effectiveness?

☐ How can I effectively respond to "RFPs"?

☐ Why should marketing efforts to any target precede proposal writing?

☐ What are the keys to producing winning exhibits?

WHAT IS A PROPOSAL?

A proposal is a document that sells a target on the basis of your firm's ability to perform specified services. The proposal must indicate that your firm understands their needs and has the willingness, facilities, human resources, management experience, and track record to support the tasks to be performed, minimize the burden on the client, and ensure that the delivery of services or final product is of high quality.

Proposals can be seen as being comprised of seven sections, including the following:

1. *Background information.* This brief section introduces who is proposing what to whom. It may also reflect some prevailing conditions or important observations.

2. *Statement of the problem.* This section provides at a minimum a brief history of the need or problem as diagnosed by the proposal writer and the occurrences or events that led up to the present situation. The concluding paragraph in this section should highlight the objectives of the proposed engagement and might quite literally begin with the phrase "Our objectives in undertaking this assignment" or "We hope to accomplish. . . ."

3. *Methodology or approach to be followed.* This section highlights the underlying rationale for the activities, steps, and/or procedures that you feel are necessary and proper in the professional execution of the proposed engagement. This is an important section because the client must comprehend and agree with your approach to solving the problem as defined in the previous section as a prerequisite to initiating the engagement.

4. *Scope of work.* This section spells out the precise tasks and subtasks that you propose to undertake, including their initiation, sequence, and completion time. This section is traditionally bolstered by a program evaluation and review technique (PERT) chart or other supporting exhibits that illustrate to the client your proposed tasks chronologically (see Figure 17–1).

5. *Expected end product.* This section is generally brief and concise. It describes what the client can expect as a result of being provided your services. It also helps to alleviate any client misconceptions as to what services and what results should be expected.

6. *Management and staff resources.* This section introduces and describes the project director, who has overall responsibility for the successful execution of the project and has the power and authority

FIGURE 17-1
Monthly Work Plan

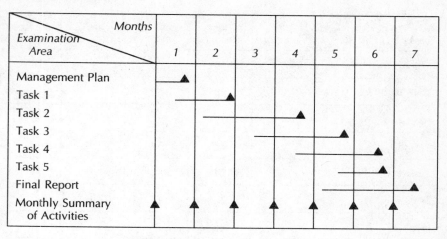

Examination Area \ Months	1	2	3	4	5	6	7
Management Plan	▲						
Task 1		▲					
Task 2				▲			
Task 3					▲		
Task 4						▲	
Task 5						▲	
Final Report							▲
Monthly Summary of Activities	▲	▲	▲	▲	▲	▲	▲

▲ Deliverable

to redirect, extend, or otherwise represent the firm per contractual agreement; the project manager, who is responsible for the day-to-day control and management of the project, continuing client liaison and handling of all staff assigned to the project; and project staff, who may be called on to perform various professional services. This section is traditionally bolstered by a project organization chart, a staff days allocation chart, and biography sketches or resumes (see Figures 17-2 and 17-3).

FIGURE 17-2
Typical Project Organization

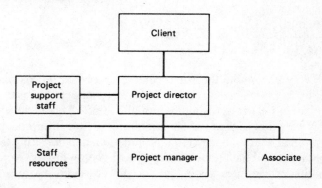

FIGURE 17–3
Project Staff Days

Tasks \ Title	Project Director	Project Manager	Asso-ciates	Staff Consultant	Total
Management plan	4	8	3	—	15
Task 1	2	20	12	6	40
Task 2	4	32	28	16	80
Task 3	2	16	14	8	40
Task 4	5	24	12	9	50
Task 5	2	20	12	6	40
Final report	2	9	4	—	15
Monthly summary	2	8	3	—	13
Total	23	137	88	45	293

7. *Cost.* This section is sometimes referred to as the *cost* proposal and is delivered as an attachment to the main body of the proposal. This section includes an elaboration of all direct labor costs, other direct costs, labor overhead rate, general and administrative expenses (that can be billed to the client, if so agreed), travel expenses, profit or fee, and total project cost. This section is supported by detailed line extensions and summaries of all cost categories. Footnotes to the cost computations are also given, including cost reduction activities such as use of client office, space, and equipment.

THE CLIENT-CENTERED PROPOSAL PROCESS

Now let's examine the client-centered proposal process and how it contributes to the submission of an effective, on-target proposal. The first step (see Figure 17–4) is handling the initial contact. This includes defining the client's perception of the need situation, probing for information that you must have in order to fully understand the situation, and nurturing the climate in which both you and the client will freely and openly discuss expectations. It is in this first crucial area that a "go" or "no-go" decision must be made.

FIGURE 17-4
Client-Centered Proposal Process

1. *Handle initial contact*
   Define client's perception of need situation
   Surface expectations
   Probe for "must-know" information
   Make "go-no-go" decision

2. *Develop client-centered data bank*
   Learn the nature of client's organization, market, and industry
   Organize your experience in handling need situation

3. *Plan for initial meeting*
   Establish objectives
   Prepare meeting guide
   Information to verify
   Information to obtain
   Evidence to bring along
   Define role(s) and responsibilities of proposal team

4. *Conduct initial meeting*
   Verify preinterview research
   Define situation
   Surface expectations

5. *Prepare client-centered proposal*
   Assign responsibilities
   Schedule worksteps
   Prepare outline
   Expand outline with first draft
   Review draft with review board

6. *Review and present proposal to client*
   Schedule meeting
   Rehearse presentation
   Identify likely questions
   Conduct presentation
   Seek commitment to proceed

7. *Follow up as required*
   Assess situation
   Assign responsibilities
   Make contacts
   Determine reasons for winning (or losing)

If a "go" decision is made, the next step is to develop a client-centered data bank. This means assembling data or information that enables you to understand the nature of the client's organization, market, and industry (see Chapter 7, on researching markets). You must then organize your experience in handling this particular client need situation.

The third step in the process is to plan for the initial meeting. Spell out your meeting objectives. Also, prepare a meeting guide that includes information that must be obtained, information that must be verified, and any supporting props or presentation materials that you must bring. The roles and responsibilities of your proposal team should also be determined during this planning session.

The next step in the client-centered proposal process is to conduct the initial meeting with the client as a prelude to proposal preparation. During this meeting you should verify your preinterview research and more precisely define the need situation with the client. At this time you should again seek to bring both your and your client's expectations to the surface so that both parties are working in synchrony.

The next step is preparation of the client-centered proposal following the seven proposal sections as outlined earlier in the chapter. An effective technique for ensuring proposal success, however, is to review both your proposal outline and first draft with an in-house review board. The review board can consist of staff or associates that closely scrutinize and criticize every component of the proposal. This will greatly strengthen your final product to be delivered to the client.

The next step will be to present the proposal to the client and review all questions and concerns. You may wish to rehearse your presentation and identify likely questions in advance. If you are going to be assisted in your proposal presentation, the presentation roles and responsibilities should be worked out in advance. The presentation should be client-centered—proceeding at the speed in which the client can comprehend what is being proposed. Your goal is to obtain the client's approval and commitment to the project so that you may initiate the engagement in a timely manner.

A final step could be called *follow-up*, in which the overall situation is assessed, responsibilities assigned, and key contacts made. It is at this time that you should also reflect on your reasons for winning (or losing) this bid for new or additional business.

One consulting engineering firm is in the practice of calling its marketing team together to assess the operations in the areas of proposal preparation and presentation. The team leader asks each member to answer the following questions:

1. What was the "tie breaker" in each winning situation?
2. What percentage of submitted proposals won in each of the functional disciplines? Was there a consistency in the wins for each area?
3. To what extent did the oral presentation play a role in the situations in which they did not succeed?
4. Is the competition doing something new or different?

Lively and penetrating analysis then ensues.

MECHANICS FOR WRITING

It is best to write a detailed outline of the entire proposal. A checklist for the mechanics of writing the proposal is presented in Figure 17–5.

An effective alternative to undertaking the time and effort required to produce a proposal is to prepare a concept paper.

FIGURE 17–5
Mechanics of Proposal Writing

Develop a checklist to ensure that all desired information is included.
Use no more than four (4) indentations, for example:

I. Section	(1)
A. Subsection	(2)
1. Topic	(3)
a. Subtopic	(4)

Make sure that no one section is more than three (3) times the length (number of pages) of any other sections.

Begin each new section at the top of a new page.

Put the complete table of contents, exhibits, and appendix lists in the front of the proposal.

Use spacing to facilitate reading.

Attempt to limit lists to six (6) items, and at maximum nine (9) items.

Include exhibits in the text adjacent to where the exhibit is cited.

Tell the readers what you're going to say, state what you want to say, and tell them what you've said.

Avoid acronyms, abbreviations, and colloquialisms; write to an uninformed audience who has moderate interest.

Limit sentence length.

Use graphs and charts freely, but make sure that they are able to stand alone.

CONCEPT PAPERS: A SHORTCUT TO THE PROPOSAL PROCESS

The concept paper is a marketing tool and significant aid in moving the client further along in the selling process. Concept papers are relatively easy to prepare, inexpensive, and most importantly, well-received by clients. They lie some place between offering a client or prospect a full-blown proposal and making an informal suggestion about services you can provide.

The primary purpose of the concept paper is to determine if the prospect has significant interest in pursuing with you a solution to a problem. It is a valuable marketing tool as it helps you to "test the waters" before committing more substantial resources in pursuit of new business development.

A concept paper should define what you perceive as the prospect's or client's problem and offer a methodology or approach that will provide an effective solution. If favorably received, it can lead directly to a professional service engagement or to the development of a more formal, detailed proposal.

Steps in Development

The first step in developing a concept paper is, of course, to meet with the potential client to discuss his or her situation. The conversation should focus on the problems and needs of the client; you should maintain an air of concern with confidence. Have available your corporate qualifications statement or supporting literature and copies of any previous reports or project materials that illustrate your capabilities in the desired skill areas.

The second step is to achieve an understanding of the task to be undertaken to achieve the client's goal. With the client present, it is useful and effective to sketch out roughly the desired end product or products or the future scenario after your services have been provided.

Step three involves suggesting to the client that perhaps it would be best if you were to "put some thoughts down on paper" to help put the problem and your proposed solution in perspective. Your role should be to gently guide the prospective client while not pushing or hard-selling the client to make any type of decision now.

Putting It Together

Generally, the concept paper ranges between three and five pages, preceded by a one-page cover letter. It should convey that these are your initial thoughts after spending some but not an inordinate amount of time on the problem. Regardless, a well-developed concept paper should indicate that you understand and have expertise in handling the client's problem. The concept paper should be developed as an *end product;* it is not intended to be modified, revised, or otherwise reworked. However, the concept paper does not deal with the scope of work, project management, or project cost.

Five-Part Approach

An effective format for concept papers consists of the following approach:

- Cover letter
- Statement of the problem
- Objectives
- Proposed methodology or technical approach
- Summary

Cover Letter. The cover letter begins with a short paragraph confirming your interest in helping the client solve a specific problem. This is followed by a second paragraph that alludes to the concept paper that follows. This paragraph also informs the client that the concept paper is a document designed to stimulate discussion and perhaps further examination of the problem areas.

The third paragraph of the cover letter thanks the client for expressing interest in your firm and for the opportunity to submit the concept paper. It never hurts to mention that you look forward to working with the client, as this helps foster an atmosphere of team work and cooperation.

Statement of the Problem. This section should not exceed two paragraphs or roughly one-half page of double-spaced typing. It succinctly states the history or background of the problem as well as any present considerations. The information contained in this section should be derived largely from what the client has expressed to you or what you have learned in close observation of the client's problem.

Objectives. The objectives section should be brief and to the point and can be completed ably by bulleting three to five major project objectives. These objectives may encompass what you believe to be important in addition to what has been expressed by the client.

Proposed Methodology or Technical Approach. This is the longest and most involved section of the concept paper. It includes a task-by-task description of your proposed approach in undertaking to solve the client's problem. Normally, two to three pages in length, it should convey your proposed methodology or technical approach in specific terms in chronological sequence. Project organization, staff allocation, and other charts and diagrams, however, are not necessary and are not recommended for inclusion in a concept paper.

Your proposed methodology or technical approach may also be enhanced or shortened by the use of bullets, outline format, or other word-saving devices. The last bulleted item should offer the client some form of closure vis-à-vis a final report, the installation or enhancement of an appropriate system, or other desirable outcome.

Summary. The summary need not consist of more than a one-paragraph wrap-up that restates the client's problem and highlights or emphasizes the effectiveness and benefits of your proposed methodology or technical approach. The summary should conclude by restating that the approach outlined in your concept paper represents your preliminary thoughts, which may be further developed, i.e. ". . . based on our understanding of your current problem . . ." or ". . . of this potential opportunity . . .".

The summary paragraph should also reiterate the unique experience and capabilities of your firm in providing an effective solution to the client's type of problem.

RESPONDING TO RFPS

Larger organizations, and local, state, and federal governments issue requests for proposals (RFPs) to which a large number of competing firms may respond. Especially in the case of federal government contract proposals, you have reduced flexibility in determining the scope of work, level of effort, and presentation. You must be able to follow the required format and content prescribed by the contracting agency.

In preparation for writing a solicited proposal, five basic steps must be taken:

1. Analyze the RFP for the technical requirements of the job. (Few bidders do this.) Carefully observe any timing, sequencing, logistics, reporting, or other requirements. Also, fully familiarize yourself with the evaluation criteria: you must score high to win.

2. Make detailed notes of any inconsistencies or problems you may encounter in reading and interpreting the RFP. These should be resolved before writing the proposal. Feel free to call the designated agency official or contracting officer to discuss these problems.

3. In all cases attempt to make personal contact with the agency or organization. Despite the stipulation that you should not make personal contact, touch base with agency officials who may be taking part in the initial review or with key staff members. It certainly helps if you are known. Try to elicit information on what type of firm the agency is seeking and how the job should be done.

4. Conduct background research on the problem, and review the goal of the agency or organization. A good source when bidding on U.S. federal contracts is the *Catalog of Federal Domestic Assistance,* which is offered on a subscription basis through the Office of Management and Budget, Executive Office of the President, Washington, DC 20503. State and local governments may have similar documents available. Be sure to inquire.

5. Contact any neutral individuals working in the content area for information they may be able to provide. This might include individuals

within the specific agency or organization who have responsibility in some other program area. Whenever information about the agency or organization is obtained, it is of potential value to your proposal writing effort.

Also for each "we will do" statement that you make, add a corresponding "you will receive" benefit. This will help the proposal reviewer follow your approach.

SUBMITTING THE PROPOSAL

In general, submit the finished proposal in advance of the deadline. This is advantageous for several reasons, including the following:

1. Your proposal may stand out more clearly than those received during the last-minute avalanche.
2. Your proposal stands a better chance of being reviewed more fully.
3. Your peace of mind can be maintained.
4. You have effectively saved time and expense through early submission.

When responding to requests for proposals, always use plain paper and simple binding—nothing elaborate. Avoid fancy type or format. When submitting the proposal to an agency, be sure to obtain a receipt.

About 7 to 10 days after submission, call to make sure that everything is in order and ask whether you can be of further assistance.

ENHANCE PRESENTATION BY PRODUCING EFFECTIVE EXHIBITS

Producing effective exhibits that are designed to either stand alone or enhance proposals (as well as articles or other written material) increases your overall marketing effectiveness.

Free-Standing, Self-Explanatory Exhibits

Design exhibit graphs and charts so that they are free-standing and self-explanatory. Free-standing means that any reader can understand information or data presented without having to refer to any accompanying text. The self-explanatory feature means that all row and column headings are free of confusing or ambiguous abbreviations. Also, any keys, legends, directions, equations, or footnotes in support of the information are contained within the exhibit or on the actual exhibit page so that the reader need not look elsewhere for this information.

Further, any computations or data presented must be consistent and follow a logical mathematical progression so that the reader can quickly ascertain how information was derived. For example, if the figures in "Column 5" are the product of figures in "Column 3" multiplied by those in "Column 4," then this should be clearly indicated.

List Sources of Information

For charts and exhibits that contain information from secondary sources—not directly based on your own research or findings—be sure to list the name of the source or publication, the publisher, the publisher's city and state, the page number, if possible, and the year in which the information was published or compiled.

This reference source can be listed on the bottom left-hand corner of the exhibit page and footnoted to the column in reference. In a similar manner, other reference sources can be listed under the first one cited and, again, serve as footnotes to the information contained in the chart above.

Serve the Uninformed but Interested Third Party

Exhibits should be prepared so that an uninformed reader, someone who has no previous knowledge of your work or the topic area, can easily and successfully examine your exhibit. Technical jargon—the principles for effective action letters are in force here!—acronyms, and coding should be avoided if at all possible.

The form and layout of the exhibit should be pleasing to the eye—comfortable margins, use of wide space, centering, and balance. If you find yourself cramming too much information in one exhibit perhaps it would be best to create a second exhibit or to eliminate nonessential information.

An exhibit that can be understood by an uninformed, but interested third party, guarantees that your primary target audience will find the exhibit easy to examine and will appreciate your production efforts.

State Assumptions When Necessary

When presenting any type of numerical analysis based on incomplete or insufficient data be sure to state your assumptions via footnotes so that the reader is not misled into thinking that the information provided is based upon established facts or substantiated primary data.

For example, a marketing analyst for a database management information consulting services firm had difficulty in pinpointing the mean age of a certain vendor's microcomputers, currently operating in the defined trade radius. She was able to overcome this problem by gathering information on the vendor's annual unit sales in the trade radius and then by making basic assumptions about the number of units still in force based on known factors of obsolescence and replacement. In preparing her exhibit, she included a footnote accompanying her data that read as follows: "Assumes normal replacement rate of 3.5 years. . . ."

Label and Date

Finally, make sure that the label or title of your exhibit is appropriate and adequately describes the information being presented. There's nothing worse than a carefully prepared exhibit headed by a misleading or awkwardly phrased label. Other supporting information should also be contained on the exhibit page. This should include the date the exhibit was prepared, who it was prepared by (can be an individual or organization), and any other point of reference useful to yourself and others using the exhibit in the future.

SUMMARY

The proposal is a key marketing tool of the trade. Proposal development and submission can be a costly process; thus an internal system for identifying where and when proposals will be written must be established. Although writing a good proposal cannot in itself secure new business, writing a bad one can surely result in loss of business.

The format and packaging of the proposal often play a significant part in influencing the target that a service is needed or that your firm represents the best of all firms submitting proposals.

The target is generally concerned with the professional's knowledge of the specific industry, previous or present clients served in that industry, and the personnel who will be directly engaged on the project. The prospect probably will have only marginal interest in a professional's firm history, organization, or training programs. A small engagement may require a proposal that is merely an elaborate action letter and only a few pages in its entirety, whereas a large engagement may require 20, 30, or 40 pages. In any case, proposals should contain as much information as needed to cover all important points effectively and efficiently.

Unfortunately, many professionals begin their real marketing efforts when they start work on the proposal, or concept paper, whereas marketing efforts should be initiated long before. Your *ongoing* efforts to favorably influence targets of opportunity is part and parcel of the development of a successful proposal. In the final analysis, the best proposal is no proposal because you're wired!

CHAPTER 18

Desktop Publishing as a Marketing Tool

Many large professional service firms have long had their own in-house publishing facilities. As Gutenberg gave the Western world the power of the press, rapid advances in desktop publishing extend that capability to even one-person service firms.

Much has been written on desktop publishing hardware and software systems and supporting peripherals. Steering clear of the technical aspects of desktop publishing, we will examine its use in supporting a client-centered marketing approach. This chapter will focus on how you can use desktop publishing as part of your overall marketing efforts and will provide answers to the following questions:

☐ What are the three primary reasons why every professional service marketer needs desktop publishing?

☐ When does it make sense to use, but not own, desktop publishing equipment?

☐ What are the steps in buying a system?

☐ What are the marketing benefits of publishing a newsletter?

☐ What are some regular newsletter features you can employ?

THE BIG THREE

There are three compelling reasons why most professional service providers who are not already employing desktop publishing should do so.

1. *Quick response to market opportunities.* Much as the personal computer enables you to customize proposals, reports, and articles, desktop publishing contributes to your effectiveness and responsiveness. Consider the implications of a direct mail package with components that appear typeset, yet which have been altered slightly for variations in the needs among subgroups within the market niche.

   A barrister (lawyer) in Glascow, Scotland, responding to new changes in the tax laws used his desktop publishing system to speedily, yet professionally disseminate a two-page flyer that both announced the changes and explained how businesses should prepare to meet them. By rapidly preparing and distributing this professional communication, he was able to generate new business among five recipients to his mailing.

2. *Leverage.* Desktop publishing enables you to leverage everything you currently have on disk for repackaging and reuse. For example, if you have written articles, independent of whether they have been accepted for publication, you can reformat and reproduce them as monographs, special reports, or other tailor-made, stand-alone information reports that enhance your overall marketing program.

   A management consultant in St. Paul, Minnesota, reviewed his file of final reports to clients following consultant engagements and identified four reports that were generic in nature. By removing specific details applying to clients, generalizing the reports to a larger audience, and reformatting each page with his desktop publishing equipment, he was able to produce four salable reports, ranging from 18 to 36 pages. He priced the reports at $15.00, $19.00, $23.00, and $27.00 respectively. Using his desktop publishing equipment he also produced a handy, one-page order form, which he included with his usual direct mail campaigns and other professional correspondence.

3. *Customer expectations.* Perhaps the most compelling reason why desktop publishing is essential is that during the 1990s, excellence in the style, appearance, and layout of the printed word will become the norm. The best firms will adhere to the highest standards, and the best customer will expect finely printed documents.

USE BUT NOT OWN

To benefit from desktop publishing equipment you don't have to own it. The threshold for a system purchase is between 10 to 12 pages per month. For example, if you publish a monthly eight-page newsletter, would like to convert some of your previous customer reports into generalized reports, or undertake any other combination of activities that averages 12 pages per month, then buy your own system. As with most emerging, multiuse technologies, once you own the equipment you begin to find additional uses for it and shortly thereafter, don't see how you lived without it.

Acquiring Outside Desktop Publishing Services

If you run a small firm, have little experience employing near typeset pages, or have an expected use per month of ten pages or less, for the time being it pays for you to retain outside services rather than buy your own system.

Identifying service firms that offer desktop publishing is becoming easy. Many businesses listed in the yellow pages under "word processing," "secretarial," or "graphic services" list desktop publishing as part of their advertisement. The services offered and the accompanying prices often vary widely so you will have to do comparison shopping.

One way to get started quickly is to assemble some of the key documents you would like to have converted to near typeset. Also round up other firms' materials that you would like to emulate. Submit this package to three to five desktop publishing services and ask each how they would handle such assignments, what their billable procedures are, and how much they would charge for the completed work.

In addition to asking about costs, you will want to cover the following brief checklist of questions when making contact with service providers:

☐ How do you base your charges for mechanical, design, and creative work?

☐ What other types of customers have you worked with?

☐ Do you have samples?

☐ Is your printer capable of producing camera-ready output?

☐ What would you charge for a specific job (describe it)?

Some services base their fees by the page, while many others base their fees on an hourly rate. At first, you may feel more comfortable with a per-page fee because you will be able to estimate better what the total charge for a job will be. As you become more adept at working with the desktop publishing service, and as you are able to develop an ongoing working relationship, the hourly charge may become more attractive.

Hourly fees can range from $12.00 per hour (small service firm, operating out of a private home) to $85.00 an hour or more. Even at the high end, it is far cheaper than the traditional route of retaining a graphics designer and offset printer.

OWN AND USE

The purchase of a system should be part of a progression. You don't want to jump from not being computerized straight to desktop publishing; it is too much of a leap and you are liable to have thousands of dollars worth of equipment staring you in the face months after the purchase. Ideally, your office already has at least one IBM- or IBM clone-based system, or a Macintosh-based system, which you or your staff routinely use for word processing among other functions. To achieve near typeset quality output with professional-looking graphics requires software in excess of $1,000 up to $5,000 or more.

You can get hopelessly confused with the variation of hardware and software options. With a hard disk system several relatively inexpensive software programs are available. To master the basics requires only a couple of hours. To become proficient, however, requires at *least* 3 to 6 hours of training, followed by 15 to 30 hours of practical follow-up, with quite a bit of frustration and trial and error thrown in for good measure.

The key to selecting a system is having a clear idea of which features are most important to the type of work your firm produces and the type of documents you would like to distribute. Important features to look for when considering a system include the following:

1. Number of fonts and the increment of sizes available
2. Flexibility in setting up tabs
3. Flexibility in laying out columns
4. Ability and ease in handling long documents
5. Ability to import files from other software including graphic programs
6. Compatibility with other software you may be using

The Printer Makes It All Happen

The development of the laser printer was essential for the emergence of desktop publishing as a widely available marketing tool. As of this writing, laser printers that can offer progressively finer printing resolutions are available at prices from $1,000 to $5,000. The Macintosh systems are more user friendly than IBM PC-based systems, particularly in regard to printer linkage. The PC-based systems are catching up particularly in light of direct management and other user-friendly software and may soon achieve parity.

A viable alternative for many first-time users is to forego the purchase of the laser printer in favor of outside service firms. In-house you handle everything except final printing, which can be done for you for as little as $1 to $2 per page.

A financial planner in New York found that in addition to number crunching, her PC was able to turn out near-typeset quality documents that impressed clients and prospective clients. By using a prepared format for her six-page proposals to prospects, she was able to convert a larger percentage of prospects into clients.

Her clients were particularly impressed when they received their individual financial analysis in near-typeset form. Many clients commented on the fine appearance of her analysis and felt particularly pleased that they were able to find such a highly effective financial advisor. Not surprisingly, this helped to stimulate her client referral system.

No System Is an Island

Your desktop publishing system can't be an isolated station that remains separate from your office's other technologies. Your system must do more than simply plug into the wall—it should do work to support *all* aspects of your marketing and office operation. Accept as a given that any equipment you buy will require careful integration and an extended training program to ensure that you get maximum return from your investment.

ENTER THE NEWSLETTER

In our previous edition of this book, published in 1985, we concluded that for most professional service firms the time and effort in producing a newsletter was inordinate. The advent of desktop publishing has changed all that. Depending on the size of your firm, you can effectively produce a quarterly newsletter, and perhaps a monthly newsletter, ranging from two to eight pages. Keep in mind however that eight pages of material per month is the same as writing a complete book in the course of a year.

A Targeted, Tasteful Document

A newsletter enables you to offer high-quality executive communication to clients and targets at relatively low cost. While your newsletter may directly generate new business, like all of the other marketing tools discussed, it is part of a client-centered marketing system that favorably and continuously keeps your name in front of those people who can reward you with new business or speak favorably about you to others.

The newsletter is a particularly effective print-related promotion vehicle in support of your prospecting efforts (see Chapter 24). While you may not be able to call continuously on all prospective clients as frequently as you would like, once a legitimate prospect has been identified, the newsletter enables you to maintain contact—beneficial for converting prospects to clients in the future.

Your newsletter should perform three important functions:

1. *Provide information.* Your newsletter can tell your targets and other recipients what the important trends are in their industries. Tell them what is occurring that they must know about and how it might impact them. The information that you have already compiled in maintaining your client-centered marketing approach represents ideal fodder.

2. *Education.* Is there an important resource or new guidebook your targets would appreciate hearing about? By providing the name, address, and ordering information of available literature or other material of interest to your targets, you will be regarded as offering a valuable resource. Consider using anecdotes and minicase histories of how firms in the industry of your targets were able to solve particular problems. These don't necessarily have to be firms that you have served.

3. *Promotion.* By providing your targets with information and educational materials you have earned the right to devote some space in your newsletter to promotion of your firm. In a quiet, matter-of-fact manner, recount some recent activities or what you were able to achieve for clients. Also review "Good Topics for News Releases" in Chapter 15 for items for your newsletter. If you have expanded your services, relocated, hired new staff, purchased new equipment, won an award, or spoken at a convention, include this.

A Canton, Ohio, management services firm found that a four-page newsletter distributed every other month worked best for them. They maintained a low-key approach in promoting themselves, concentrating more on providing solid information that targets would appreciate receiving. The in-house editor reported that she received several favorable responses from recipients and, over the course of two years, did not receive any negative responses of any sort.

Developing Regular Features

Whether you are issuing your first newsletter or your fiftieth, the development of regular features will help to decrease the problem of what to include. Each of the following may contribute to the information, education, and promotion functions of your newsletter:

- *Message from the president, branch, or managing partner.* This message could reflect trends in the targets' industry since the last newsletter, mixed with personal opinion, forecasts, or other observations.

- *Capitol Roundup.* Provide information on current or proposed legislation, new rules, or regulations that may impact clients. If your practice area is national in scope, you will find that many clients appreciate getting the "early word" on these developments.

- *Client of the Month.* Profile one of your clients, particularly something the client has done that represents bold, progressive, or insightful thinking. You will make 12 good friends in this coming year by establishing this column—the 12 clients featured.

- *Industry Calendar of Events.* List the important meetings, seminars, conventions, and symposiums of interest to members of your target niche. This kind of data is often derived from other publications; nevertheless, recipients will appreciate it listed concisely in your newsletter.

- *Technical Report.* Offer a roundup of new equipment or technology that supports clients' efforts. Your assessment of the effectiveness of new equipment, costs, and potential applications will be appreciated by many recipients.

- *Interview.* Present a 150- to 300-word interview with principals of your firm; movers and shakers in the industry; association executives; magazine, journal, or newsletter publishers in the industry; key clients and client staff people; and other outside experts. The interview—in question-and-answer format—provides a visual break from normal text layouts.

- *Reprints, Excerpts, and Adaptations.* Reprint information that first appeared in another print medium. You will have to secure permission, which in most cases is readily granted. This is a wonderful space-filler!

Here are some additional features that can keep your newsletter fresh, vibrant, and in demand:

- Cartoons or captions appropriate for your targets.

- Synopses of meetings held in the target's industry.

- Indication of your availability as a speaker.

- Community or regional information including youth employment programs, charitable and civic programs, and fund-raisers for the arts.

- Sketches or photos that illustrate accompanying text.
- Graphs or charts depicting industry trends, financial changes, and other noteworthy developments.

The task of identifying newsletter material is not difficult—once you get started. You can assign a junior staff member the responsibility of clipping articles and keeping an eye open for newsletter items, from which you can make final selections.

System Maintenance

Each issue of the newsletter must be assessed for balance, readability, and adherence to the firm's *goals and objectives* in producing the newsletter in the first place. A newsletter that accurately conveys your firm's goals and objectives is a marketing tool worth maintaining.

One firm views its newsletter as a *continuing dialogue* with clients and potential clients and strives to anticipate what clients would like to be receiving. As with direct mail and other forms of targeted communications, the list of newsletter recipients must continuously be updated and purged as necessary.

Generally, one person must be responsible for its publication and distribution, though others will have input. One- and three-page newsletters are possible but have drawbacks. A one-page newsletter doesn't allow much depth of coverage of topics or features—clients and recipients may not save the issues. A three-page newsletter—three single sheets joined by a staple, or two sheets folded over to make four normal-sized pages with the back sheet for mailing—appears a bit unbalanced.

Two-, four-, and six-page newsletters are popular. Two pages (front and back) or four pages (two 11" x 17" pages folded over) are simple in design and easy to mail. A six-pager, which equals a four-pager with insert, is a popular option. At the eight- or ten-page level, you have to consider the difficulty in maintaining reader interest.

Many direct mail and newsletter pros suggest having your newsletter three-hole punched to encourage recipients to save them. The most popular page size in the United States remains 8½ x 11 inches. A larger page doesn't fit into notebooks or file folders. A smaller page may get lost among other documents.

A law firm based in San Juan, Puerto Rico, sends its four-page newsletter (folded once) in a 9 x 6 inch envelope. The envelope decreases the possibility of the newsletter being mangled in the mail and tends to make its distribution seem more important to recipients.

Another firm, which distributes a six-page newsletter and includes a "client of the month" feature, prints 2,000 copies—1,700 for their own distribution and 300 for the client being featured. The rationale is that the client will distribute their copies to its own customers.

PATIENTS APPRECIATE THEM, TOO

If you are a doctor, dentist, or firm offering any type of health services, a newsletter makes excellent sense now more than ever. As with other professionals, the promotional aspects of the newsletter must be kept low key, if included at all. By simply providing consumer health care information, you establish yourself as a knowledgeable healer.

One Boston physician began a two-page monthly newsletter, heavily adorned with prevention measures for patients. After a few months, people who had seen the newsletter were calling to receive it, even though they had never met the doctor himself.

As many as three out of ten physicians currently offer or are contemplating offering their own newsletter. The doctor in Boston felt certain that his newsletter was a more effective promotional vehicle than any other medium he had tried.

In medicine, as in other services, association-based and private publishing services that offer generic newsletters are on the increase. These publications are written, produced, and shipped to service providers who then add their own copy, name, and address on the final page (or final two pages) so that the publication appears to be their own unique creation. The cost ranges from $500 to $700 for 2,000 copies, with more attractive rates for larger orders. Additional cost is then incurred for adding the customized page(s).

Regardless of the size of your firm or practice and the service you provide, desktop publishing is a marketing tool whose time is here.

CHAPTER 19

Building a Brochure That Works

A brochure serves as a central source of printed information to existing and potential clients. Although there are no absolutes about what the brochure should contain, most experts agree that an effective brochure contains information on your firm's (1) history, (2) philosophy, (3) organizational structure, and (4) service areas. Your brochure should enhance your image as it literally represents you on paper. It should also be designed to project uniqueness—to make you and your firm stand out from all of your competitors.

In this chapter we'll help you to answer the following questions:

☐ Keeping in mind the need to produce a client-centered brochure, what type of information do prospective clients want to gain from your brochure?

☐ What is a quick way to determine which type of brochure is right for you?

☐ Should you attempt to complete your brochure in-house?

☐ What are some of the design options available in the development of your brochures?

NOT AN EASY JOB

Production of your firm's brochure is a complex undertaking and one that requires significant effort. Figure 19–1 illustrates 14 brochure formats including the standard format (see Format 9). For most professional service firms, it is desirable to lay the groundwork for the brochure but ultimately rely on outside assistance for completion. In undertaking this project, you may ask yourself (1) what target you wish to reach and (2) what message you wish to offer.

A CLIENT-CENTERED BROCHURE

Most professionals as well as other business entrepreneurs end up producing a brochure that perhaps supplies ego gratification but does not adhere to the needs of the client and hence does not follow the client-centered approach. *Your brochure is not for you, it is for your clients and prospective clients, and should be developed for their needs.*

FIGURE 19–1
Brochure Formats

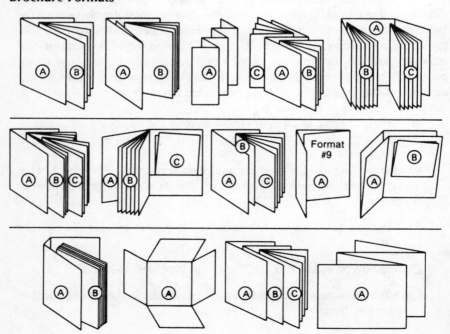

Your firm's brochure, in the words of Ted Eisenberg, president of Ted Eisenberg Associates, "is, in effect, an expensive, illustrated calling card."

A prospective client will certainly be interested in the basic information about your firm, including history, philosophy, organization, structure, and service areas. Specifically, however, the client will also be interested in learning about:

1. The qualifications of your staff.

2. The quality of your service.

3. The size and location of your offices.

4. The range of your services.

5. Your firm's reputation.

6. Your firm's experience in specific industries.

7. Others who have used your services.

8. How long you've been in business.

For the small practitioner with little change in personnel, it is permissible to include pictures, a short biography, and other references to yourself or staff personnel. For slightly larger firms, this may be a costly mistake as personnel turnover, the addition of new partners, or other developments quickly render the brochure outdated. To alleviate this problem, you might try producing separate flaps describing individual staff that can be inserted into jackets within the main section of the brochure.

SCANNING THE COMPETITION

A quick way to determine what type of brochure will be right for you is to assemble the brochures of competitors and study their efforts. If your collection is not large, this would be a good time to write for and acquire the brochures of others so that you can more properly undertake this exercise. Writing to firms outside your trade area will probably yield better results than writing to those firms that are direct competitors.

After you've assembled at least ten brochures of other firms, carefully review those features that appeal to you. There are hundreds of factors to consider. The following list represents a mere subset of all the options available in developing your brochure:

Use of flaps, pockets, foldovers   Use of color
Dimensions of brochure   Use of testimonials
Quality of paper   Use of bulleted sections
Use of pictures   Action photographs
Weight (affects mailing cost)   Spacing
Staff biographies   Heading, titles
Client lists   Captions
Sketches   Style of print
Number of pages   Association affiliations

CONSULT A SPECIALIST

You will eventually need to turn over the development of your brochure to a marketing or graphics specialist. The key to effective use of an outside resource is to produce a rough prototype of your desired end product. Sketch out on several pieces of paper the layout and content of each brochure page. If photographs are to be enclosed, leave space accordingly.

In the selection of outside assistance, try to seek marketing or advertising professionals who have experience working with firms similar to yours and ask to see samples of their work.

The cost of your brochure can range anywhere from $1,000 to $2,000 per page, and it is the number of pages—not the number of brochure copies printed—that is the single biggest cost factor. The proper size or number of pages is a trade-off between your budget and what is needed to deliver your message effectively. (*Note:* A single sheet with material printed on both sides counts as two pages.)

An effective brochure works hard at marketing and promoting your firm. Thus the dollars invested in producing a high-quality product can be dollars well spent.

CHAPTER 20
Advertising for Results

Advertising has traditionally been defined as any paid form of nonpersonal presentation of ideas, goods, or services by an identified sponsor. Advertising can involve the use of a wide variety of media, including magazines and newspapers; outdoor posters; signs; novelties, including calendars, desk blotters, and the like; direct mail; and publications such as catalogs, directories, circulars, bulletins, brochures, and pamphlets—to name but a few.

In this chapter, we'll focus on the following questions:

☐ What are some of the objectives of advertising?

☐ What type of information should be included in an effective professional service firm advertisement?

☐ Why is it difficult for a small firm to effectively establish an advertising budget?

☐ What are the steps to hiring outside help?

☐ If you hire an individual or agency to assist with your advertising plans, what are some of the control techniques that you should adopt?

☐ What are some techniques for stretching your advertising dollar?

THE OBJECTIVES OF ADVERTISING

Advertising as it relates specifically to professional services is the use of direct mail and advertisements in magazines and newspapers to present both informative and persuasive communications that are designed for and targeted to present clients, potential clients, and all other public groups or individuals who you have decided you would like to reach and influence.

E. Jerome McCarthy, in *Basic Marketing—a Managerial Approach*, says that "every advertisement and every advertising campaign should be seeking clearly defined objectives." He lists basic advertising objectives, some of which any individual advertiser would logically be seeking. Here is an adapted version of McCarthy's list for use by professional service firms:

1. Aid in the introduction of new services to specific targets.
2. Assist in the expansion or maintenance of an identified market.
3. Enhance the firm's personal selling efforts. (Move a target from one stage of the buying process to the next.)
4. Keep your firm's name before targets.
5. Provide information regarding the availability of new services and possible application of other services.
6. Provide contact with identified targets when personal selling cannot be undertaken.
7. Aid in the establishment of the firm's image.
8. Induce the target market to take swift action (i.e., get in touch with your firm).
9. Help clients to confirm their decision to hire your firm.

A properly executed advertising campaign can potentially affect the profitability of your firm. It can also round out your total marketing program. Similar to other tools, however, it cannot in itself substitute for provision of excellent services, sell the services per se, or create and maintain relationships.

WHAT TO ADVERTISE

In a survey recently conducted it was learned that business professionals believe advertising will make the public more aware of the availability of services, and advertising can be tastefully used.

The information that can be effectively advertised includes:

Availability of services

Specialization in certain areas of the profession

Specialization in certain industries

Date firm was established

Announcement of changes in personnel, location, or hours

HOW MUCH TO SPEND?

The hallmark of an effective advertising program is to prepare a budget well in advance of actual expenditures. Although it may have little meaning to your particular situation, historically, advertising expenditures have equaled approximately one percent of total revenues for professional services, based on Troy's *Almanac of Business and Industrial Financial Ratios*. Thus a firm receiving $1,000,000 in annual revenue could be expected to spend approximately $10,000 per year on advertising. Advertising in newspapers and business periodicals can be very expensive, however, and the smaller firm may find the cost to be prohibitive.

Focusing on a hypothetical firm with revenues of $1,000,000 per year and an advertising budget of $10,000, the task of allocating that $10,000 (or other amount if so chosen) soon becomes tricky. Decisions must be made regarding Yellow Pages advertising, brochures, and business cards, as well as directory listings and miscellaneous printed materials to accompany mailings.

It is difficult to advise professional service firms on how much to spend for the creation of an effective advertising program. For an established firm, an effective brochure and statement of qualifications is a must. For the younger firm whose personnel, qualifications, and even address is constantly changing, this can turn into a major project.

Initially, a business needs more advertising to gain recognition. Regardless of the age of the firm, the decision to establish an ongoing advertising and promotion budget must be based on realistic projections of anticipated annual gross sales.

THREE WAYS TO SPEND ON ADVERTISING

Three methods of determining an advertising budget are as follows:

1. *Percent of sales method.* Stable firms often take the previous year's sales figure as a base for the upcoming year's advertising budget. The advantage of this method is that it is traditional and convenient and also subject to quick review in light of sales gains or decreases. However, this method looks backward and may perpetuate last year's mistakes. This method also tends to overlook increased costs of media and production.

2. *Task method*. This is based on concrete estimates of the job to be done. The firm sets a specific goal and then spends when and where needed to achieve that goal with every dollar at its command. This assumes confident, responsible, and imaginative management of the entire marketing plan and also involves constant awareness of advertising themes and trends and what the competition is doing. Most budgets are based on a mix of percentage of sales and task method.

3. *Empirical method*. This method assumes that the way to determine the optimum to spend on advertising is to actually run a series of tests at different levels of advertising. This method requires detailed planning, patience, and a large budget for testing. It also requires discipline in not drawing hasty conclusions.

As one might readily determine, none of the three traditional methods of budgeting successfully provides the small firm with a clear indication of how much to spend on advertising.

SEEK OUTSIDE HELP

To maintain a consistent advertising and promotion program with effective follow-up, it might be necessary to hire a part-time creative person or to employ an agency to perform similar tasks. It is best to avoid the do-it-yourself approach to advertising.

Working with an advertising agency basically requires the gradual building of a relationship. Trust is built over time through continuing and open communication. This begins when you work on your first advertising campaign together. At this time, you will need to come to agreement on:

1. *Objectives*. What do you want to accomplish?
2. *Market*. Whom do you wish to reach?
3. *Message*. What do you wish to convey?
4. *Media*. Which media will be used?
5. *Evaluation*. How will the results be evaluated?

The ad agency (or free-lance professional) whom you choose, like you, is marketing a professional service. Your evaluation and selection of an agency mirrors the selection process wise clients undertake before choosing *your* services.

The first step in your decision process is determining what you want the agency to accomplish for you. This is represented by a written list of key items spelled out in detail:

- Do you want the agency to offer advice and serve as consultant on issues beyond advertising?

- Is the agency being retained only to produce and place advertising copy?

Full-service firms, as well as many firms in general, can offer most, if not all, of what you want from them. You are the one however, who must spell out what that service offering will be.

The second step in choosing the right agency is to reverse the process and prepare a list of what you intend to provide to the agency. Share this list with prospective agencies and pay close attention to what they expect from you.

We recommend calling on three to five agencies, based on referrals you receive from other people or professional associations. You will want to know the same things about the agency you choose that prospective clients want to know about you before retaining your services: items such as history of the firm, names of top management and key account executives, number of employees, total annual revenues, the firm's experience in dealing with professionals like you, list of client references, and other background information that will aid you in your ultimate selection.

The temptation to simply have advertising agency representatives visit your firm and put on a dog and pony show is enticing, but don't fall for it. Most professionals can make a pretty good 30-minute showing at your office, but what is in their portfolio doesn't equal what you can see by visiting their offices. You want to visit agencies on their own turf to make a first-hand assessment of their facilities, the way they run their offices, and the scores of other visible and not so visible clues as to what type of partner you may be retaining.

When finally choosing an agency, don't be afraid to trust your instincts; they are there for a reason. The size or prestige of the agency is not nearly as important as:

- How effective they will be with you.
- A good working relationship.
- Their deep understanding of your needs.

Over the course of your relationship with the advertising agency selected, feel free to take an active role:

- Show and use your knowledge of advertising techniques when directing the firm or individual you hired to help discourage misuse of funds or overspending.

- Seek an individual or firm that has handled similar accounts and has good media contacts, including editors, writers, graphic artists, photographers, and typesetters.

- Always ask for a copy of any ad that is run. This will serve as a double check against late publications, poor-quality results, and mistakes.

- Create an advertising file to include masters of all ads run, a copy of the actual publication, and an invoice for all expenses incurred. This will help greatly in adjusting the budget for current spending and in projecting for the next year.

STRETCHING YOUR ADVERTISING DOLLARS

To stretch your advertising dollars, consider these suggestions:

1. *Seek complementary advertising*. If an advertisement of yours says "located next to Brown's Hardware," make sure that Brown says he is located next to you in his advertisements.

2. *Seek exchange of services*. If a local editor needs your services, you might barter for an ad or two in that editor's publication.

3. *Check with your professional trade association*. Consult them to see if they offer assistance through standard industry copy, formats, logos, and the like.

Many professionals overlook the fact that they can obtain a directory listing for free or a very small fee by creatively seeking various printing sources in their area. For example, in metropolitan areas where the telephone directories are larger than an inch thick, you will often see a community telephone directory consisting of local merchants. Chances are that placing a display advertisement or one-line listing may bring in additional business.

Other places where your firm may be listed include Chamber of Commerce directories, neighborhood telephone directories, community business guides, merchant desk blotters, minority business directories, shopping center guides, local business circulars, and other privately published directories of business and professional services. Your local librarian can quickly identify numerous directory sources of interest.

For the small professional service firm, the effective use of advertising—in light of cost, time, and effort required—may prove to be an inordinate task. Through the use of the other nonpersonal promotion tools discussed, even a small firm can establish a system that effectively places the name of the firm in front of appropriate targets at a reasonable cost.

PART FIVE

Personal Promotion

The next step in the profitable marketing of professional and consulting services involves favorable promotion of *yourself* and your services. Promotion consists of the numerous activities involved in educating your targets, stimulating inquiries, and managing your image. Personal promotion consists of first-person, "press-the-flesh" activities that you undertake to favorably present your capabilities and ability to meet needs. Personal promotion is eye-to-eye or elbow-to-elbow contact and the use of personal letters that are action oriented.

The key objectives of promotion, based on principles of a client-centered marketing, leveraging approach are to:

☐ Favorably bring the firm's name before "targets of influence" and "targets of opportunity," and educate and inform same.

☐ Establish and maintain a sound and working relationship with the press and industry publishers of your target group and establish a reputation as an expert and willing source of information.

☐ Improve the firm's public and professional image by systematically gaining exposure for principals and professional staff in appropriate media.

☐ Develop and distribute client-centered, informative literature about the firm.

☐ Create a competitive difference by differentiating the firm's image with its targets.

☐ Stimulate and create inquiries from your firm's targets.

☐ Portray the benefits of your firm's services in an appealing fashion.

In the six chapters that follow, the focus will be the critical factors of personal promotion that yield the highest payoff for professional service marketers.

CHAPTER 21

Leveraging Your Memberships

Visit any metro area and attend a local meeting of the Red Cross, International Rotary, Les Femmes Chefs D'Entreprises Mondiale, or other civic, professional, or charitable groups and undoubtedly, you will meet many of the area's most successful professionals. Successful professionals know that giving of their time freely is an excellent way to be of service to the community and to help build the firm. After completing this chapter, you'll know:

☐ Why it is important to join charitable and civic organizations.

☐ The names of at least three national groups that have chapters in your area.

☐ The key criterion for joining an organization.

☐ Why joining any organization will be fruitless if you do not meet and remember targets of opportunity and influence.

☐ The two best leadership positions to hold in any organization.

EARNING A POSITION OF LEADERSHIP

Civic organizations such as the Chamber of Commerce, Scouts, and the YMCA afford professionals ample opportunity to rub elbows with key community and business leaders and jointly work on solving local, civic, public, and business problems. In marketing your professional services it is often assumed that you are fully competent in your practice area. The important thing is getting known throughout the community and getting known among your peer group in other professions. Earning a position of leadership in a high-visibility organization is an excellent way to be of service and, as a by-product, promote your services. By volunteering your services and assisting civic and charitable organizations, targets of opportunity, and influence come to know you as a person and then feel comfortable in using you as a professional or in referring your services to others.

Joining and serving can only be effective if you "pay the price" required to gain a leadership position in the organizations and associations in which your *targets* belong. You are leveraging off the reputation of the organization, and the lead time necessary to begin to receive "benefits" can range from 6 to 18 months. Many professionals don't stand their ground, drop out, and never realize that benefits of leveraging were just "around the corner."

An unsophisticated marketer joined an organization and unrealistically expected to generate new business simply as a result of attending various meetings and becoming known. After nearly two years he resigned his membership and concluded that joining organizations "just isn't for me."

A resourceful consultant joined an organization comprised of decision makers in her targeted prospective client organizations. She sought and was appointed to the new member committee. Serving in this capacity, she met all new members, and during the course of the screening, interviews, and subsequent new member activities, developed sound relationships that eventually led to opportunities to discuss ways of serving them.

Later she was appointed to the program development committee. While serving in this capacity, she contacted the community's leading speakers to determine if they would speak to the organization. Within a year, she had first name acquaintance with several community influentials.

JOINING TO SERVE WITH A PURPOSE

Memberships in professional and civic activities need to be closely monitored to determine whether marketing results in addition to personal satisfaction are being achieved. Otherwise, joining can be a serious drain on the firm in terms of time and energy. Because every community is different and the interplay of political, social, cultural, and religious spheres varies from time to time, a customized joining-serving strategy must be prepared.

It is essential for professionals to continually analyze organizational contacts for relationships that should be developed, paying particular attention to younger executives on their way up. This approach must be balanced, however, with the realization that the only organizations that one should join are those in which one has a genuine interest and desire to serve.

Numerous strategies abound for the successful penetration of charitable and civic organizations. One way is to seek specific offices. For example, the role of activities chairman is a coveted position in many groups because one can gain a high degree of visibility and have virtually unlimited access to key people in one's market and practice area.

If there are two or three or more partners in your firm, you can match partners' personal interests with the firm's goals. Thus Jones may join A, B, and C groups, whereas Brown joins D, E, and F. You may choose to join C, F, and G, thereby increasing your firm's visibility in organizations C and F and maintaining some visibility in all seven.

If you do not meet and remember targets of opportunity and influence and they do not remember you, the act of joining any organization will be fruitless from a marketing standpoint. Some professionals maintain card files on individuals when a key contact is made. Information is continuously added to the card file as it is obtained.

Making targets of opportunity and influence remember you is a delicate matter. The best way is to respond professionally and completely when asked about your profession and not to "oversell." If your commitment to and involvement with a charitable or civic association is extensive, you may rightly expect that you will become known and remembered by many of the right people.

Figure 21–1 depicts how an accounting firm in Calgary formalized community involvement among its professional staff.

DO THEY USE YOUR SERVICE?

The most effective technique in joining with a purpose is to seek out that group whose members routinely use your type of service. Marilyn Coopman offers management training seminars. Using Gale's *Encyclopedia of Associations,* she identified a group called Meeting Planners International. She called them long distance and found that Meeting Planners International had a chapter in her city. She obtained membership information from the national headquarters, and then made contact and ultimately joined the local chapter.

Marilyn discovered that she did not have to be a meeting planner herself in order to join the association. She joined in an "associate" capacity. Many types of associations maintain different categories of membership. This greatly increases their membership rolls and provides a service for members who then are in a position to interact with potential suppliers and service providers.

FIGURE 21–1
Sample Community Involvement Planning Form

West District Office Community Involvement Plans Period _____ To _____		
Name of Organization	Date Joined	Number of Meetings

Over the next year, Marilyn faithfully attended sessions, volunteered to serve on committees, and at one monthly meeting was featured herself. Because the members of the local MPI chapter began to know her, and were impressed with her presentation, she received several phone calls from meeting planners (members) who were interested in having her present one of her seminars within their respective organizations.

Describe Your Plans to Become Active in the Organization. Include Committees, Offices, etc. and Expected Timeframe	Estimated Time Requirements

Robert Zyblut, a diversified financial services broker for an internationally recognized brokerage firm, volunteered to chair a suburban Maryland society of certified public accountants. Each month Robert identified and secured a speaker for the group; wrote, edited, and distributed a newsletter; and became a one-man information clearinghouse.

As you might guess, many of the CPAs retained Robert as a counselor for their personal investments and referred others to him. Though his time and commitment to this group were substantial, Robert found that on balance, he had generated more new clients in a shorter time period than in his entire professional career.

GROUPS, ANYONE?

Why not take the time right now to identify six organizations in your community that interest you. The following list offers the names of groups that may commonly be found in your area. A local phone call will yield membership information.

Active Corps of Executives	Jaycees
Audubon Society	Jewish Community Center
Boys' Club	Kiwanis
Business and Professional Women's Club	Labor Party
	Lions
Cancer Society	March of Dimes
Catholic Youth Organization	Masons
Chamber of Commerce	Optimist Club
Children's Hospital Committees	Parent-Teacher Association
	Public Television
Conservative Party	Regional Park Authority
Democratic Party	Republican Party
Easter Seal Campaign	Rotary Club International
Elks	Salvation Army
Explorers	Scouts
Fraternities (professional)	Toastmasters International
Garden Club	United Way
Goodwill Industries	Volunteer Services
Heart Fund	Walkathon
Historical Society	Wilderness Society
Independent Party	YMCA, YWCA

CHAPTER 22

Speaking: An Underused, Undervalued Tool

Many local organizations such as the Chamber of Commerce and civic and charitable associations actively seek speakers. Yet the program chair of these groups often must scramble to find an interesting speaker. If you give a good presentation as a volunteer speaker to local groups, and are in fact able to influence the audience, rest assured that you'll be contacted by individual members at some point in the future regarding professional services. In this chapter you'll discover:

☐ What is the best way to position yourself to be invited to an organization.

☐ What type of letter should be sent describing your topics.

☐ What tips should be followed to increase your effectiveness.

☐ The key components of delivering a speech from a script.

☐ Why you should make sure your presentation is taped.

☐ Why you should always provide "handouts" for the audience.

POSITIONING TO SPEAK

The best way to position yourself to be invited to speak to a local organization is to be a member of that organization. This strategy ties in with the need to join charitable and civic associations.

The authors have consistently applied this principle and in the last years we have spoken to the following groups, of which one or both of us have been members:

International Platform Association
Institute of Management Consultants
Greater Washington Society of Association Executives
Active Corps of Executives
American Marketing Association
National Speakers Association
International Toastmasters

SPREADING THE WORD

An excellent way to spread the word that you are available for seminar presentations is to type a one-page letter explaining who you are, a little about your background, and a one-line or short paragraph description of three to five topics on which you are prepared to speak. This letter could easily be photocopied and distributed by your clerical staff to 50 to 100 groups in the local area. As a result of this mailing and depending on how well known you are in the community, two to five speaking engagements may be generated. A sample letter appears in Figure 22–1.

For this or any other mailing, it is wise to send a second letter or to have someone on your staff make a follow-up phone call to each of the organizations receiving your letter. This reinforces each recipient's knowledge of your desire to speak.

Even when contacting meeting planners who represent small groups, consider that the people whom you are trying to reach are very busy. Whether they love your topics or are indifferent to them, chances are they may not get back to you in a timely fashion, or may not get back to you at all. The onus is on you to ensure that your initial communications are received and understood. As with personal selling, the incidence of your speaking to a particular group will be highly dependent on the level and adequacy of the interpersonal communication between you and the meeting planner.

Most groups meet on a regular basis for a fixed number of hours and have a fairly well developed meeting agenda. Within those givens however, it is your responsibility to take charge for suggesting which topic might be of particular interest to the group and why, how much time you think will be necessary to deliver the topic, whether or not there should be a question and answer period, and other particulars of your presentation.

The more precisely you can describe what you wish to present to the group and the more empathetic you are to the group's needs, the higher the probability that they will invite you to speak.

FIGURE 22–1
Sample Speaker's Letter

Alvin I. Speakeasy
Consultants Unlimited
10 Orator Avenue
Wichita Falls, TX
(817) 444-4444

Dear Meeting Planner:

Your organization may have need for a speaker with my experience and qualifications. I am a management consultant serving businesses and government agencies since 1982. I have had numerous speaking engagements and written several articles on effectively managing a business.

My most frequently requested topics are:

How to trim expenses when there's nothing left to trim

How to attract, motivate, and retain young executives

The record-keeping aspects of managing your own business

Eight ways to save on advertising expense

Incorporating a firm

How to find the right consultant for your business

How to prepare a loan package

Your interest is appreciated. Feel free to call me at the number above to discuss any of the topics listed.

Yours truly,

Alvin I. Speakeasy

DELIVERING YOUR TALK LIKE A PRO

Volumes have been written on how to deliver an effective speech. The most effective speakers are those who operate without a net—they don't read from a script or use notes. These are pros who speak for a living, have delivered their speeches over and over and know exactly when to pause, when

FIGURE 22–2
Deliver Your Talk Like a Pro—Working from a Script

A. *Make a readable script*

1. Make the script readable at a glance. Use double space or even triple space on just one side of the paper.
2. Use a speaking language.
3. Underscore key words.
4. Put a diagonal mark between words where you want to pause.
5. Number your pages.

B. *Settle the butterflies*

1. Take a few deep breaths while waiting to be introduced.
2. Review your opening lines.

C. *Approach with enthusiasm*

1. Come on with enthusiasm and smile.
2. If you have a lot of notes and props, have them at the lectern ahead of time.

D. *Open with style*

1. Take about five seconds to arrange your notes before you start to speak to let yourself and the audience relax.
2. Say "Good morning" or whatever is appropriate.
3. Thank the person who introduced you. Tell why you're glad to be there.
4. Compliment the audience in some manner.

E. *Read the way you would talk.*

1. As you finish a page, slide it across to expose the next one. Look at the audience, pause slightly, and they won't realize you did it.
2. Scan a few lines ahead so you can look at the audience frequently as you speak.
3. Pause now and then as though thinking of the right word even though it's right there in the script.
4. Talk directly to the audience as much as possible and talk to people on the left, in the middle, and on the right.
5. Don't lean on the podium.
6. If you fluff a line, ignore it or laugh it off.

F. *Use humor—but watch out*

1. One-liners are the safest humor for the nonprofessional.

G. *That parting smile*

When you come to the close of your talk, put your notes aside, look out at the audience, moving your attention from one group to another while you give your closing statement. Tell them how great they were, your wishes for their success. Put your arm up as a farewell greeting and smile as you walk off.

to get a laugh, and when to come on strong. Since most professionals don't speak for a living, it is advisable to prepare notes or, if necessary, to work from a script.

We recommend jotting down a few key words on a page rather than producing a full-blown script. Each key word generally is "worth" two to five minutes of presentation time. To deliver a thirty-minute speech, ten key words on a page, each representing about three minutes of presentation time, ideally, are all the notes that you need.

If you are more comfortable with a script, then by all means have it typed in abnormally large print with plenty of spacing so that you can find your place easily when you are standing at the lectern. The chart in Figure 22–2 will carry you through the process of delivering your talk like a pro, particularly if you are using a script.

HONING YOUR EFFORTS

When you start to get requests to speak, you will need additional information such as the size and setup of the meeting (see Figure 22–3). A checklist of items you should determine to increase your effectiveness on the day or night of your presentation is given in Figure 22–4.

QUESTIONS FOR REFLECTION

Bruce Harrison, president of the E. Bruce Harrison Company, a public relations firm based in Washington, DC, suggests reflecting on the following 20 questions in your quest to become an effective speaker:

1. How do I get people to listen?
2. When do I start speaking?
3. How do I handle nervousness?
4. What am I doing here?
5. How do I handle questions?
6. How do I handle hostile questions?
7. Should I be aggressive?
8. How do I take charge?
9. How do I not sound defensive?
10. What if I am not an expert?

FIGURE 22–3
Meeting Room Setup

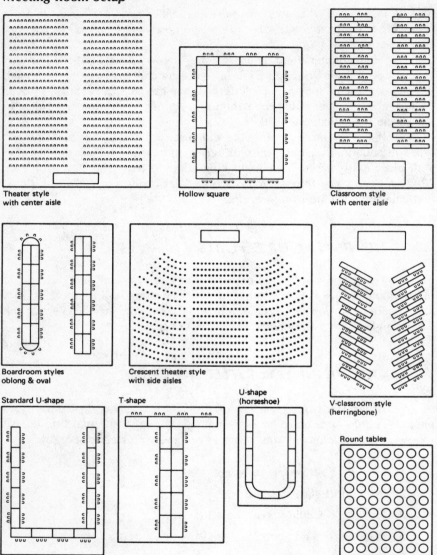

Theater style
with center aisle

Hollow square

Classroom style
with center aisle

Boardroom styles
oblong & oval

Crescent theater style
with side aisles

V-classroom style
(herringbone)

Standard U-shape

T-shape

U-shape
(horseshoe)

Round tables

FIGURE 22–4
Checklist for Effective Speaking Engagement

☐ Size of room	☐ Audiovisual equipment
☐ Setup, staging	☐ Surrounding rooms
☐ Number of attendees	☐ Temperature
☐ Program length	☐ Lighting
☐ Sound system	☐ Audience composition

11. What if I don't know the answer?
12. What if the question is dumb?
13. Should I smile more?
14. Should I try to gesture?
15. Where do I look when I speak?
16. Where do I look when I am not speaking?
17. If I can't comment, what can I do?
18. Can I fudge the facts?
19. How can I tell if I am scoring?
20. Where are the restrooms?

OPENING NIGHT

Here are some guidelines for making your presentation:

1. *Posture* should be erect and poised.
2. *Hand gestures* should be made mainly between the shoulder and the waist and be appropriate to the material presented.
3. *Body movements,* if made, should be stable and appropriate to the material.
4. *Vocal production* must be audible to the size of the audience.
5. *Vocal intonation* should be varied.
6. *Vocal rate* should be appropriate to the size of the audience and the material presented.
7. *Articulation* must be clear and precise.

8. *Delivery* should have few or be absent of audible pauses.

9. *Eye movement* should make contact regularly with the audience.

10. *Approaching and leaving* should be deliberate.

GET YOUR SPEECH ON TAPE

Every speaker should insist on being taped while making a presentation to a live audience. Why? There are five reasons:

1. *Taping affords personal review of the presentation.* There is no better way to review your performance than to hear exactly what you said and how you said it, on tape.

2. *Each tape is potentially salable.* Tape cassette producers, manufacturers, and distributors can professionally edit your tape, supplying voiceovers and transition passages that can result in a salable cassette. Keep in mind that there are other audiences similar to the one to whom you spoke. It may pay for you to be able to repeat your presentation on tape.

3. *The tape transcript is salable.* Don't overlook the value of marketing the tape transcript to members of the group you addressed. Professional societies frequently offer tape transcripts from symposia and seminars that they have sponsored to those members who were not able to attend or who wish to have a written record of what was said in the speech.

4. *The transcript can be converted into articles.* Frequently, a transcript of as few as three or four pages lends itself to being turned into an excellent article. Every writer finds it easier to start from an established base and make editorial changes than to face four blank pages and begin writing. With longer transcripts, it may be possible to extract several excellent articles, which in turn can be used to promote your speaking career and earn additional income.

5. *Use tapes to get other speaking engagements.* After your speaking engagement has been taped, you can extract a 5- to 10-minute passage that can be used to develop demonstration tapes for distribution to other meeting planners. What better way for them to assess your speaking skills than to hear a passage from a live performance?

HELPING THE AUDIENCE
TO REMEMBER YOU

Distribution of article reprints or other written material along with the speaking engagement "provides the audience with an opportunity to secure the correct name and address of the speaker." Thus it always makes good sense to hand out something with your presentation. On the other hand, don't attempt to make a sales pitch or sales presentation; merely speak on a topic of interest and do your best. Never expect a speech or presentation to bring instant results. Altman and Weil, a professional services consulting firm, reports that it received telephone calls from targets who heard a member of the firm speak several years previously.

One way to ensure participation of the group to whom you speak is to offer a handout that contains some blank spaces and fill-in-the-blank-type exercises. By giving members of your listening audience a task to perform (i.e., making the handout that they have received more complete), you raise their interest level and the probability that they will retain your material.

Consultants and professional service providers who frequently speak to groups find that it is a faux pas to circulate all of your handouts at once. With a three-page handout, for example, distribute each page as your presentation progresses. This reduces the incidence of attendees flipping the pages and getting ahead of you. It is a little more effort to circulate the pages individually, but doing so provides a brief vocal pause for you, and a mental pause for your listeners. In advance, you can share with the meeting planner the manner in which you wish to have seminar materials distributed.

Your decision on whether to seek speaking engagements as a personal promotional tool hinges on your ability to be interesting and have something worthwhile to say to a group composed of targets of opportunity or influence. If you've never spoken before a group, you have a unique experience in store. Everyone is nervous at first, but shortly you may find speaking quite exhilarating. Before continuing, on a separate sheet of paper make a rough copy of your own speaker's letter, modeled after Figure 22–1. Then turn it in for typing, because it's ready for mailing!

CHAPTER 23

Using Video as a Marketing Tool

The video explosion is here; with each passing day more offices and more homes are equipped with VCRs. Popping in a video tape has become as easy as popping bread into a toaster. The frequency of professionals appearing before camera, whether for their own in-house video production, cable TV, or local or national television program, is on the rise. They appear as a public service, to enhance stature, and to gain increased exposure. In this chapter, we'll explore:

☐ How to make contact with producers.

☐ Why coaching is so important.

☐ How to meet the press on your own terms.

☐ The "Rule of FIVES".

YOUR BEST TOPICS FOR THE CAMERA

The topics that you would be qualified to present before the camera right now are the same topics upon which you speak, write, and counsel clients. Virtually every professional service provider who gives speeches or writes articles, as well as many who have not, could make a well-qualified, compelling presentation before the camera.

If you are a financial planner, speak on financial planning for women; if a tax consultant, address what new tax changes mean to personal income. With the emergence of narrowcast programming (as opposed to broadcast) your topics are in demand on plenty of channels and plenty of shows.

MAKING CONTACT WITH PRODUCERS

Most of the guidelines already presented on making contact with editors and meeting planners apply here. The producer of a local talk show wants to know what your qualifications are for the topic you are suggesting. Your task is to prepare a short, punchy, compelling cover letter, followed by a small press kit which includes:

- a good 8x10 inch black and white glossy photo of yourself
- your firm's brochure
- any articles by or about you
- any articles on the topic you will be addressing
- a question and answer sheet prepared for the show's host

If you have been on previous shows or have participated in professionally produced videos and therefore have a video of yourself, indicate it on your cover letter. Don't send it initially; producers get dozens of them each week. If you have only an audio cassette mention that. An audio cassette still helps a producer or show host to get an idea of what type of guest you would be.

Identifying all of the shows, both television and cable in your local area, on which you might possibly become a guest, is not a difficult task. Your local library contains community, regional media, and broadcast directories that list the names, addresses, and phone numbers of stations; the names of producers, show hosts, and shows; times; and in some cases, target audiences. It makes good sense to watch or listen to at least 30 minutes of any show you would like to be on.

GET SOME COACHING

Not everyone is a natural talk show guest, and particularly if you think you are, it pays to get some coaching in advance. Being interviewed before the camera is not the same as successfully engaging in a one-on-one encounter or presenting live to a group. The camera confines and distorts, overaccents and underaccents, instantaneously and without passion.

When giving an interview on television and radio (or with the print media for that matter) *you* must take charge of the interview so that you optimize how you come across and hence, your marketing impact. An appearance on camera can bolster or detract from your overall marketing goals. A coach can help you take charge and achieve your desired effect.

MEET THE PRESS—ON YOUR TERMS

Former television news and radio reporter Karen Kalish, now head of Kalish Communications, a Washington, DC, communications firm that provides training programs and instructions on being effective on camera, offers the following observations and advice: Giving an interview is a glorious opportunity to get your point across and gain high visibility. It's a chance for exposure and free advertising, to inform the public and express your views, and to put your firm in the minds of targets. You have to be prepared, however, and that means going into an interview with an agenda.

Kalish says that your goal is to make three positive points in any interview situation. Interviewers will have their own lists of questions to ask, but you can't assume they'll be the "right" questions. *You* have to become an initiator—you can't let the interview proceed without making your three positive points. Your positive points are your "islands of safety," places you can hop to when asked a question you don't want or one that doesn't fit your game plan.

"Positive" means offer your points with positive words, not negative ones. Volunteer information to make a positive point. You have a job to do during the interview: to score with your three positive points. Allow nothing to keep you from that goal.

In addition to positive points, you must have examples. These are stories or anecdotes that illustrate your positive points. Perhaps you remember the story Michael Dukakis told during the Bush-Dukakis debates of the little boy who couldn't participate in sports because his father couldn't afford medical insurance. Kalish observes that few people remember anything *else* that was said during that debate, although Dukakis lost "points" for many other reasons. Stories are what people remember. Be an anecdotal interviewee.

A caveat: There is no such thing as "off the record." Don't say anything you don't want to hear broadcast on television or radio or to see in print. Giving background information is fine, and there may be some reporters/hosts/interviewers you can trust. But as a general rule, consider everything you say to be *on* the record.

Sitting to Win

Kalish recommends that you sit with your derriere well back in the chair and lean forward, which gives you an air of authority and credibility. If your back is resting against the back of the chair, you are too comfortable; sit alert and forward. Your hands should be free to gesture, not be glued to the arms of the chair or to each other. Gesturing makes for a more interesting interview and lets off nervous energy.

When the engineer asks for a voice level, state your name, spell your last name, and give your title and the subject of the interview. That simple technique communicates a world of information: they get their voice levels and the correct pronunciation and spelling of your last name and your firm. Also, the reason for the interview is made clear.

Act as if the microphone is always on. Several years ago, someone ended a show on Friday by saying, "Have a good weekend." Then the audience heard, "That should hold the bastards!" His mike was still on.

What to Wear
Clothing is important. Blues, greys, khakis, and pastels look the best. Kalish says that the uniform for men is blue suit or sport coat, pastel shirt, with a red or burgundy tie. Shoes should be polished and repaired. Socks should be above the calf. Beware a shiny forehead and 5 o'clock shadow.

Women should wear a suit or dress with sleeves, no flashy prints or sexy frills, and closed-toe shoes.

Don't wear anything that will distract from what you're saying. No white, black, yellow, green, or brown anything, or chunky, shiny jewelry.

Bridges and Highways
How do you get from an answer that doesn't make a positive point to one of your positive points? By using bridges, those phrases that get you from their answer to yours. Use such phrases as the following:

"It's important to tell your viewers (listeners, readers . . .)"

"I'm also frequently asked . . ."

"For instance . . ."

"You should also know that . . ."

"That's not my area of expertise, but I do know that . . ."

"If you don't know an answer," Kalish advises, "say so and promise to get the answer as soon as possible." And do. Even though the viewers won't actually know if you obtained the answer or not, your commitment to obtaining the answer to a question will score points for you.

Occasionally, and depending on the subject, you may get hostile or difficult questions. Don't get rattled, or repeat any negative sentences or phrases. Correct misinformation quickly, and go on to state a positive point. If you are asked a hypothetical question, you can remind the host that you don't have a crystal ball but you "do know that . . ." and state a positive point.

What if you receive several questions in a row? Kalish says to pick the one *you* want to answer and then ask the interviewer to repeat another question. It's not up to you to remember his questions.

Your Interview Rights

You have many rights where the media are concerned. When a reporter (from either broadcast or print media) calls you for an interview, rather than the other way around, there are ten questions you should ask:

> What is the topic?
>
> When is the interview?
>
> Where will it be? (If you prefer it at your office say so.)
>
> How long will it take? (Twenty to thirty minutes is plenty for radio or TV; print may take a bit longer.)
>
> Who will conduct the interviews? (Then watch, listen, or read something by this person to gain familiarity with his style.)
>
> Will you be alone or on a panel?
>
> If on a panel, with whom?
>
> Why you?
>
> Will it be aired live (unedited) or taped?
>
> When will it air?

The more you know, and the more prepared you can be, the better the interview you will offer. When a radio or print reporter calls and wants to do an interview on the phone, get the reporter's number and say you'll call right back. In those few minutes, rehearse your three positive points, say them out loud, take a deep breath, and call back, keeping the deadline in mind.

Audiotape Every Interview. Kalish suggests this for several reasons. First, you have a record of exactly what was said in case there's any question later. Equally important, you learn from your interviews. Keep in mind those answers that you handled well, and work on those you didn't.

Consider that some of your clients or prospects may be interested in the interview, or you may want to use parts of it in a newsletter or annual report.

Remember to BEEEEP

During any interview before a camera or microphone, the magic word, says Kalish, is BEEEEP. Be Brief, Emotional/Entertaining/Enthusiastic/Energetic, and Positive. Being brief means being able to state each positive point in 20 seconds or less (radio prefers less, talk show and print a bit longer).

Since television cameras as well as radio tend to "flatten" people—make them seem bland—you have to exhibit at least two of the Es to project an interesting interview and to be remembered by the audience, who are probably distracted.

During the interview, talk naturally without using jargon, acronyms, technical terms, or alphabet soup. Kalish says to pretend you're talking to your mother. When possible, use word pictures. For example, instead of 47,000 square feet, say the size of a football field. Also, always look directly at whoever is talking, as though you were in someone's living room; don't look at the camera.

If it's ten seconds before show time and you blank out and forget your entire interview strategy, at the least smile and be open. You still have a glorious marketing opportunity. Take it.

THE RULE OF FIVES

Maggie Bedrosian is a nationally known speaker and author of *Speak Like a Pro* (Wiley, 1987). According to Bedrosian, good responses on television or videotape follow the *Rule of FIVES*.

F = Fast. Today's viewers have evolving expectations about the pacing of information. Despite our intelligence level or degree of sophistication, we all have been influenced by television where yesterday's standard 60-second commercial has given way to today's 30-, 15-, and even 5-second spot. Therefore, keep your comments short and clear. Whether in a three-minute feature or an hour-long talk show, avoid talking for long periods of time.

I = Involving. Involve your audience or interviewer as much as possible. Engage them immediately in recognizing the impact your topic has on their lives. Outline benefits or threats that will help them personalize what you are saying. When appropriate, get them to do something as they watch or soon after. Move them beyond theory into action. Draw them into your presentation in body and mind.

V = Visual. People listen and learn differently. Use visuals as much as possible to extend learning into the right hemisphere of the brain. Of course, visuals such as slides and overhead transparencies take time to prepare. As Kalish reminds, don't forget those instant visuals—your gestures, your body language, the word pictures that your voice creates in the minds of your listeners. Use symbols and pictures when possible, visuals that display only words and numbers are still emphasizing the left side of the brain.

E = *Elementary*. Do you have an elderly aunt in Kansas, and a sixth-grade cousin in Tennessee? If not, borrow one of each. Talk to these target people. The look on their faces when you try to use the normal jargon of your field will cure you. Purge jargon. Unless you are addressing only your professional peers (as in a teleconference), keep your presentation elementary. Sacrifice the image of erudite professional for the more difficult role of skilled communicator.

S = *Selective*. Remember that unless you're part of a live broadcast, film is often edited before use. Critical sections may be left intact, but don't count on it. State your positive points very concisely.

Awareness of the Rule of FIVES will help you develop your readiness and frame your responses.

Getting the Most Mileage out of Your Appearance

A financial planner from Rahway, New Jersey, appeared on a local talk show one Sunday morning. Asked by the host what an individual could do to safeguard a personal investment in a certain situation, the guest mentioned two or three good strategies and then, almost as an aside, said, "I have a ten-point pamphlet available on this very topic." The host cut in and announced that viewers who would like to receive the pamphlet could write to the guest in care of the station. The station's name and address were then presented to home viewers. (To comply with various regulations, the host did not want the guest to offer his address and phone number on the air.)

In the week following the show, 78 requests for the pamphlet came in. In the second week, 47 more came in, and in weeks thereafter, a total of 15 more. In essence, the financial planner had inadvertently created a ready-made prospect list of 140 people.

ENROLL THIS MONTH

Whether you've made the leap and have appeared on a professionally produced video or are still contemplating your first appearance, you owe it to your practice and your career to enhance your "guest" potential. The simplest way to start is to enroll in an adult education course or to hire a video coach outright. Either route represents an investment that will pay off when you make your next appearance before the camera speaking to an audience.

CHAPTER 24

Prospecting Like a Pro

A prospect is an asset to be acquired, developed, and protected. Prospecting is the task of securing appointments with qualified nonclients and is an important component in the overall client-centered marketing effort. Mastery of effective prospecting techniques enables you to maximize your available time allocated to marketing. In this chapter we review effective prospecting techniques and provide the answers to these questions:

☐ Why is it important to regard the phone as a tool?

☐ Why is "homework" an essential component of prospecting?

☐ Why is the client-centered marketing approach crucial to effective prospecting?

DEVELOPING YOUR PROSPECTING STRATEGY

The first step in prospecting like a pro is developing a strategy. Either by yourself or with a prospect strategy team composed of individuals within your firm, you want to set goals regarding the number of prospects to be identified, how you will make contact, and the frequency of follow-ups.

Once committed to establishing a prospect strategy, many firms systemize their prospecting efforts:

1. The first step is to use all referral sources and all information generated in researching the niche and other targets of opportunity.

2. Your goal is to develop a relationship with prospects, even though at this point it is just by phone.

3. The next step is to use mailings including client-centered action letters, article reprints, or possibly a concept paper depending on how the relationship is progressing.

Many firms conduct in-house seminars for their professional staff so that the staff becomes comfortable with various aspects of prospecting. Some firms assign responsibility to individual staff members (i.e., assignments based on the kinds of businesses to be contacted or geography of the prospects).

To be an effective prospector is to be effective on the telephone. There is no getting around it.

THE PHONE IS A TOOL

Waiting for the phone to ring or for clients or prospects to contact you rarely leads to successful marketing results. Getting on the phone and making things happen are the early links in the chain that lead to profitable sales success.

We have observed that most professionals prefer not to get on the phone to engage in early round prospecting and, are even reticent to use the phone to help close on a hot prospect. In our book, *Getting New Clients,* a considerable number of pages is devoted specifically to making telephone contact, working from a script, and securing appointments.

The important point about using the phone in marketing your consulting and professional services is to recognize that the phone is a tool, nothing more, nothing less. Similar to other tools that you use such as a computer, copier, or fax machine, it requires following certain procedures.

The number one rule in effective use of the telephone for marketing purposes is to relax. Your calls must convey a professional, even-paced, upbeat message. Never make calls when you are tired, have just received bad news, are time-pressed, or otherwise preoccupied.

Being on the phone is a full-time activity in and of itself. Being on the phone and staring out the window, toying with items on your desk, or otherwise diversifying your attention generally will diminish your capacity to market your services.

Find a system in which you can be comfortable and organized. Then, make sure that your phone is positioned properly on your desk or other flat surface. When making calls, and especially when receiving them, make sure that you always have a pad and pen ready so that you can keep careful notes about what the prospect is telling you. As your relationship with this prospect deepens, particularly if he becomes a client, these notes will become invaluable.

Never rely on memory or instinct regarding your perceptions of a client's needs and the information he has imparted to you. You work hard to get new clients; leverage your efforts by arming yourself with the vital information that prospects volunteer.

TARGETING THE MARKET TO BE PROSPECTED

Before attempting to generate or "work" a prospect list, it's important to profile or define the market you're attempting to penetrate and why your services meet the needs of this market. Many professionals fluctuate from day to day or week to week, continuously making halfhearted efforts to penetrate first one market, then a second, then back to the first, and then a third. They never stop to carefully analyze which market they should penetrate first. (If needed, refer back to information presented in Chapter 7 on researching new markets.)

The best way to solve this problem is to use the client-centered approach. First, identify the needs and then devise strategies to serve those needs (better than your competition can). A common mistake that all of us make is to get overinvolved in the services that we provide and forget to align our thinking in terms of what the identified target market needs. One way to determine whether your services are appropriate for a chosen target market is to learn about the experience that other professionals within your industry have had in serving this market. Another factor to consider is what developments have occurred in the political, economic, technological, business, and social environments that have resulted in new needs on the part of target markets and to match your capabilities to the needs. See Figure 24–1.

DEVELOPING YOUR PROSPECT LIST

There are several ways of developing a prospect list. Literature scans, use of industry directories, analyses of financial and operating ratios, business periodicals literature scans, purchase of industry reports, and use of consultants and attendance at specialized seminars are appropriate techniques for the busy professional.

FIGURE 24–1
External Impacts on the Client

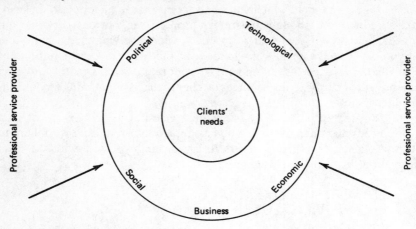

Obviously, any prospect list that you uncovered while assessing your primary or potential markets can be applied here. Frequently, annual issues of key professional, trade, and industrial magazines or newsletters contain directories of members, rosters of companies that will be exhibiting at trade shows, and other valuable lists that you can use in your prospecting efforts.

Once you have identified some of the key publications read by the market you wish to serve, you can write to those publications and determine if they sell or rent their subscriber mailing lists. You may also be able to exchange prospect lists with other professionals with whom you do not compete, who serve the same market that you do.

DO YOUR HOMEWORK

A second important step in effective prospecting is to learn about the operating characteristics of the industry or businesses—or individuals—to whom you wish to sell.

1. What in your past experience can be drawn on and used as a competitive advantage in penetrating your chosen market?

2. How have your services traditionally been accepted and used by the target market? What can you presently offer that is consistent with the changing needs of the target market?

"Homework" is often a dreaded component of effective prospecting. Yet, if you lack a minimum amount of reliable, up-to-date information about your target market, any attempts at penetrating the market will either fall completely flat or will be shaky for the first few calls as you scramble to rework your presentation, using terminology and citing examples to which prospects can relate.

Working your prospect list involves calling all parties using spaced intervals between completion of calls and start of next call. It also means calling everyone on the entire list and not letting the result of the first few calls dampen your original enthusiasm. Many professionals become discouraged because of rejection after a relatively short time. The winners, however, realize that successful prospecting means paying homage to the numbers game. Every "No" brings you closer to a "Yes."

Properly working the list also requires careful monitoring and tracking of each phone call denoting who should be called back and when, who wasn't in, who'll be returning your call, who's moved or has a number that is no longer working, and so forth. Any organized spreadsheet, chart, or notebook will do when tracking progress through prospecting. Later you can transfer the most promising prospects to the chart given in Figure 5.1.

A common mistake is to begin working the list, not keep careful records, be called away on business, and then attempt to begin working on the list again. The problems encountered, such as wondering if you already called someone, will utterly destroy your self-confidence when you make additional calls, for fear of embarrassment. The fastest way to ruin a perfectly good prospect list is to not keep a careful log of all correspondence. The way to use the prospect list to fullest advantage is to maintain an accurate, up-to-date log. It's as simple as that.

OVERRELIANCE ON TRADITIONAL SOURCES

Harold Gray, a principal with a professional service firm in a metropolitan area, had developed a knack for identifying appropriate target markets and developing prospect lists to penetrate those markets. He frequently talked with Stuart Rogers, a new partner, who had not been selling well. When Harold asked Stuart what he knew about the XYZ Industry, Stuart's reply was, "Oh, I don't think it's doing so well right now. I'd forget that one if I were you." Luckily, Harold did not overrely on traditional information sources—in this case a colleague—in determining the level of effort he would make in penetrating this particular market.

Harold bolstered his knowledge by talking to professionals in other fields, by doing some simple library research, and by reading a Department of Commerce report on the industry. He soon learned that although the industry had had several slow quarters of late, in the last six months industry sales had rebounded well. On the basis of this information, Harold decided that now would be a good time to penetrate this market and use his prospect list.

PREPARE A TIME AND MONEY BUDGET

Effective prospecting necessitates the allocation of sufficient time to work the prospect list, make sales calls, make follow-ups, and close *and* a sufficient budget in support of the sales effort. Another common mistake is to underestimate the time necessary to successfully penetrate a market and to attempt to overeconomize in support of the selling effort. The old adage "penny-wise and pound foolish" applies here. If a legitimate prospect is located across town or requires some special selling efforts, the professional must take the calculated risk that a sufficient number of such efforts will pay off.

One way to minimize expenses is to prepare a prospect list within a defined trade radius. Once your radius has been established, however, initially treat all legitimate prospects equally. Many professionals get in the habit of calling only those prospects who are very close by or will see them at a convenient time. Once your list has been established, decide realistically how much time will be required to effectively work the list and what expenses will be associated with it.

EXPECTATION OF EARLY RETURNS

Closely related to the problem discussed in the preceding section is the unrealistic expectation on the part of professionals in working the prospect list. Don't decide (after much too short a period) that the sales being generated are insufficient or that substantial early returns should be realized. Nearly every article and book on selling ever written emphasizes that prospects offer several "No's" before becoming clients.

If the world's best sales professionals require many "No's" per prospect, is it realistic to assume that your selling efforts will require less to be successful?

INTEGRATE NEW LEADS AND DATA

The proper working of a prospect list often requires the passage of time. A frequent weakness in working a list is failure to integrate new leads and data in support of a list that has been prepared and is being worked. To combat this, the proper mind set must be established at the outset of the prospecting effort.

Maintain the notion that in the course of working the prospect list, new information may be gained that may have substantial impact on the techniques and strategy you develop to penetrate this market. Sometimes you can learn something on the tenth call that is so important it's worth calling back the first nine prospects who conveyed little interest. Other times in working the list, information or leads are generated that make it worthwhile to alter your telephone presentation or, in rare instances, to forego working the list for the time being. The important point is to recognize that the target market and your penetration efforts are both part of a dynamic environment that requires flexibility and often an updating of the list.

EFFECTIVE PROSPECTING DEMANDS BEING ORGANIZED

The time spent organizing one's files and notes is an investment that pays continuing dividends. This organization effort maximizes the prospecting effort. Although we can all cite instances in which unorganized professionals achieved some marketing success, the long-term odds are clearly in favor of those who invest at least a small portion of time in getting and staying organized.

There are many ways that you can quickly and easily organize your prospecting activities. One is simply to design a prospecting form that you can use to capture valuable information for your overall efforts. This form could be designed using your PC, purchased at an office supply store, or prepared manually.

As you begin to accumulate information, the forms could be maintained on a disk, in a card file, or in a three-ring notebook. The manner in which you contain this information is up to you—what best supports your operating style and what you are trying to accomplish. Of significance, *all* prospecting data, even from prospects that you have no chance of ever converting into clients, represents valuable information that supports your overall marketing effort, provides continuity to others who may be assisting in the prospecting efforts, and should be looked upon as an ongoing function.

Files will be created; space will be taken up.

THE PERSONAL TOUCH

The final key to a successful prospecting effort is to offer a personal touch. This, obviously, is best done by being face to face with the prospect. Direct mail (discussed in Chapter 16) has its place in support of the prospecting effort. When direct mail is used as a substitute for telephone contacts and personal presentations, however, a serious mistake is being made. If you've taken the time to define an appropriate target market, develop a prospect list, and sufficiently work a prospect list, why take shortcuts once the prospect has been qualified by using the mail instead of making a personal contact?

A systems analyst firm had decided to target several industries for special attention. Staff were given the vague instructions to "locate some warm bodies" within assigned industries. A large number of names was obtained, but new business never materialized because prospects were not contacted directly.

The active approach—making the personal contact (particularly for a second or follow-up visit)—is overwhelmingly more effective than the passive approach—using the mail.

A successful prospecting effort is analogous to litmus paper. The paper doesn't work until it's dipped, and the chances are your prospecting effort won't pay off unless you appear in person and reappear as often as necessary. Following the litmus paper analogy a step further, a chemistry takes place through personal contact between the prospect and you that simply doesn't exist by phone or mail.

This chapter has presented the elements of effective prospecting and the theory that you ultimately have to "see them to sell them." Effective prospecting assures you that a healthy number of appointments can be made from which a relatively predictable sales volume can be generated.

CHAPTER 25
Mastering Personal Selling

Too many professionals still find the notion of marketing their services distasteful, and the notion of personal selling out of the question. The old ways are dying fast, however, and effective personal selling is now a prerequisite to building a long-term, successful practice.

Personal selling in the context of client-centered marketing of professional services entails face-to-face discussions with prospective users, influencers, and purchasers of your services. Your personal selling objectives include (1) contacting and obtaining additional revenue from existing and prospective clients through discussion and identification of needs, (2) retaining endangered revenue with clients who may be thinking of terminating their relationship with you, and (3) obtaining referrals and leads from satisfied clients and targets of influence such as bankers.

Supporting activities to personal selling include responding to inquiries, maintaining control and awareness, acquiring keener listening skills, developing a personal image, and establishing proper "atmospherics."

This large, wrap-up chapter to personal promotion provides answers to questions such as these:

☐ What is essential for a successful personal selling effort?

☐ What are the steps to handling inquiries?

☐ How does personal control maximize personal selling efforts?

☐ Why don't we listen as well as we should? What can be done to improve?

☐ How do personal image and atmospherics affect professional success?

EVERYONE SELLS SOMETHING

Robert Louis Stevenson once said "Everyone lives by selling something," and although many professionals do not view themselves as sales representatives, the function must nevertheless be fulfilled.

Effective personal selling requires that you have or develop the willingness and ability to sense the unmet or poorly met needs of key clients and prospects, probe for needed information without upsetting the contact, and listen to and understand the contacts' needs and expectations. It also means that you communicate persuasively in language the contact understands and, when appropriate, obtain commitment to proceed to a logical next step in the business development process.

One key to successful personal selling is having a firm conviction in your own capabilities. (Although the following may sound like a pep talk, keep in mind that effective personal selling starts with a proper frame of mind.) You may have superior technical knowledge, but this alone is not enough. Belief in yourself is transmitted to your clients and targets above and beyond what you say. Belief in yourself is important, and without it the best trained and most professional among us might as well seek another career. You must believe in yourself and that you deserve to be financially rewarded for your efforts. The enthusiasm you possess for your service is contagious; moreover, it cannot be feigned on a sustained basis. If you don't believe in what you are selling, you can't possibly expect your client or target to do so—and they won't.

When Lee Iacocca appears on television through his commercials and says, "If you can find a better built car, buy it," he is selling. When Henry Block says, "Here is another of my 27 reasons why you should use H&R Block services," he is selling. Selling is neither a dirty word nor a dishonorable endeavor. In times of economic downturn, effective selling has literally kept nations afloat. If you believe in yourself, and you believe in what you are offering, you are already in an advantageous position from which to further develop your selling skills.

Robert Bookman, a Chevy Chase, Maryland, trainer and consultant, points out the power of belief in oneself combined with persistence. Every few months Bookman calls prospects just to stay in touch and maintain the potential for a professional relationship. In eight years of calling on targets he has never had anyone request that he stop calling them. Conversely, some of those called have since become clients.

RESPONDING TO INQUIRIES

A fundamental component in personal selling, and something that will occur with greater frequency after you employ the marketing and promotion techniques outlined in this book, is response to and handling of inquiries. Figure 25–1 carries you through the process.

PERSONAL SELLING AND CONTROL

Personal control is a key element in successful personal selling. In personal selling, control of one's time, energy, and resources spells the difference between a halfhearted, limited-effectiveness sales effort and a professional, high-caliber approach.

Personal control goes hand in hand with personal awareness. There are three types of personal selling style in regard to the personal control and awareness functions: the no-control, nonaware salesperson; the no-control, aware salesperson; and the in-control and aware salesperson.

No Control, No Awareness

The professional service marketer with no control and no awareness doesn't plan in advance, yet expects to have a productive selling effort (see "Prospecting Like a Pro," Chapter 24).

No-control, nonaware marketers frequently let the effectiveness of their presentations slip. Rehearsals, brushing up, outside reading—all are relegated to the "haven't got time for that" status.

Professionals of this type are playing a loser's game, perhaps kidding themselves for an extended period or banking on a "long shot," the big contract that will salvage a poor month (or year)!

No Control but Aware

Many professional service marketers not adequately controlling their marketing effort are aware of the problem. These are people who either have let personal standards slip or never adequately developed them. No-control but aware professionals often rationalize their reasons for skipping steps in the personal selling process. If you're in this category, supplement what you've learned in this book with attendance at outside seminars, specialized courses, and programs so that your approach to selling remains fresh and viable.

In Control and Aware

Professional service marketers in control and with awareness take the time to review marketing strategies, rehearse presentations, and approach personal selling in a controlled and effective manner. This type of professional

FIGURE 25–1
Responding to Inquiries from Existing and Prospective Clients

Handling the Initial Telephone Contact
□ Project an image of interest and enthusiasm.
□ Capture the contact's initial statement and attempt to identify the nature and scope of the need situation.
□ Gather additional background data.
□ Arrange meeting details.

Planning for Personal Sales Interview
□ Organize your interview plan.
□ Select appropriate "marketing aids".
□ Prepare yourself and others who may attend.

Initiating the Interview
□ Make proper introduction.
□ Build rapport.
□ Read the contact's style and attitude.

Defining the Contact's Need
□ Determine the nature of the need situation, what's wrong, missing, required, or desired.
□ Determine the scope of the need situation.
□ Determine the costs to date and the additional costs and consequences of not proceeding.

Converting the Need into Goals
□ Review *favorable circumstances* to be retained, enhanced, or created.
□ Identify *unfavorable circumstances* to be minimized or eliminated.
□ Determine timing and form of results required.

Discussing Solution Alternatives and Agreeing on a Solution Program
□ Your need . . . we could . . . we should . . . we will . . .

Handling Contacts Concerns and Information Needs
□ Surface, define, resolve.

Closing and Seeking Commitment
□ Schedule meeting.
□ Prepare proposal, action letter, or plan.
□ Begin engagement.

knows that taking the time to maintain personal control results in maximum presentation effectiveness and overall use of time.

The effective professional service marketer is eager to learn or read about successful sales strategies. This person welcomes luck but doesn't count on it and knows that a well-executed, sustained personal sales effort is the best road to increased revenues.

LISTENING TO LISTEN

Few professional have thought about *learning* how to become a good listener. We get distracted when someone is talking, jump ahead in our minds to what we want to say next, and later blame the speaker for not getting the message across. Yet, a key tool of effective personal selling is the ability to listen.

According to researchers at the University of Minnesota, on the average, people spend 45 percent or nearly half of their communication time listening. Good listening is an active, complex process that takes knowledge of a few basic tenets and lots of practice.

Why don't we listen as well as we should? Dr. Chester L. Karrass, Director of the Santa Monica, California-based Center for Effective Negotiating, offers several reasons:

1. We often have a lot on our minds, and it's not easy to switch gears quickly to fully absorb and participate in what is being said to us.

2. We have adopted the habit of talking and interrupting too much and do not let the prospect continue even when it may be to our benefit.

3. We are anxious to rebut what the other person has said, and if we do not do so readily, we are afraid that we may forget to make our point.

4. We allow ourselves to be easily distracted because of the setting or environment in which the meeting takes place. Have you ever asked your secretary to hold all phone calls during meetings?

5. We jump to conclusions before all the evidence has been presented or is available.

6. We discount or "write off" some statements because we don't place importance on the party who is presenting them.

7. We tend to discard information that doesn't match what we want to hear or that we don't like.

Poor listeners may drop out of a conversation, erroneously thinking that they can catch up. Karrass observes that they seldom do.

YOU'RE NOT ALONE

If you're like most professionals, you may have self-confessed to being a poor listener. Lighten up—you don't have a monopoly on underdeveloped listening skills. Virtually all human being must work to improve their listening skills.

TAKE NOTES, REPHRASE, SHOUT

Particularly in demonstrating to clients that you are listening to what they are saying there are three activities you can undertake.

1. *Take notes as the client speaks*. Some professionals are reticent to do this because, for some reason, they think it is unprofessional. Yet, to make the most out of your encounters with prospects and clients, have a paper trail of what transpired and flatter the client by indicating that what he says is important, by all means, take notes.

2. As needed for your own understanding and clarification, *restate what the prospect or client has just said in your own words and get his acknowledgment that you have, in fact, understood what he said.* This technique is often preceded by phrases such as:

   - In other words, you are saying . . .
   - To put it in perspective then . . .
   - Let me see if I understand this . . .
   - So that would mean that . . .
   - Let me see if I can explain it back to you . . .

3. Third, whenever you are in doubt, shout! Don't literally shout but speak up and let the other person know when you haven't understood or suspect that you haven't understood what he has just said. It is one thing to sit there and nod your head and play the part of the cool professional, but if you don't understand what the client is saying, how can it possibly help you and your firm in the long run? Indicating that you would like more clarification regarding what the client has just said does not put you in a bad light. This same client may have explained the same thing to others who nodded in agreement and then ultimately proved that they didn't understand a word of it.

Developing good listening habits is one way to become a better communicator. Active listening improves your interpersonal skills, human relations, and personal selling capabilities. Good listening skill can also enhance your professional life.

Sooner Is Better Than Later

While most professionals would prefer not to acknowledge a fundamental reality of winning new clients, all things being equal, the more time someone takes in considering to retain your services, the less likely it is that that person will become your client.

A key component of personal selling is conveying a message of urgency. Many professionals would prefer to maintain a passive sales stance, i.e., they call or meet with the prospect, listen to the prospect's needs, present how they can meet the prospect's needs, and then wait for the prospect to make a decision. The problem with this approach is that most prospects, in a time-pressed world, have a variety of decisions to make, not just the decision to hire you or someone else in your industry. Then too, a prospect who interviews too many professionals in your industry (or who is called on by too many of them) will have an increasingly difficult time taking action and making a choice.

Your job is not to pressure or press the client to make a decision before he or she is comfortable in doing so. Nevertheless, to the degree that you can assist or prompt the client for a relatively early response, the greater the odds of your gaining more clients per prospect encounter.

IMAGE

There are two factors that so dramatically impact your ability to be effective in selling that we include them in this chapter. These include your personal image and the image of your office, which we term "atmospherics." Since you project your personal image in every sales encounter, the more you know about what image you are projecting and how that image may tend to impact a client, the more successful you will be in the long run. Likewise, anytime a prospect, or client for that matter, comes to your facilities, the observations that he makes about your physical surroundings are part of the overall impression he makes about you and your firm.

We define "image" as the "sum total of all of the perceptions your clients and others have about you and your practice." Every element of your practice over which you have discretion will contribute to the development of an image. If that image is solidly developed and consistently displayed, the task of influencing your clients and targets will be greatly enhanced.

If your image is inconsistent or nonexistent, your marketing efforts will have to be all that much more strenuous. As Robert J. Ringer says in *Winning Through Intimidation*, "it's not what you say or do that counts, but what your posture is when you say or do it." Your clients and targets expect certain behaviors and characteristics of professionals in your field. Within this area of expectation, however, it is recommended that you develop your own unique image, for this is what will differentiate you from competitors. Back in 1978 Simon Ramo, empire builder and chairman of TRW, helped to build a unique personal image by becoming an avid amateur tennis player. He even wrote a successful book on the subject.

Philosophically speaking, the image you project is you—it is not right or wrong, or good or bad. Nevertheless, people will judge you based on the image they perceive. If you are overweight, this signals to many people that you may be somewhat unprofessional. Being overweight obviously doesn't mean that you are unprofessional, but since you have to market yourself in the world as it is, it is best to understand this.

If you have sideburns of a length that does not reflect current trends, a beard or mustache, or a beard and a mustache, many prospects may judge you to be everything from "a grown-up hippie" to a "free-thinking noncon-formist." If you wear Pierre Cardin fashions, you are perceived as being an "arty" person.

No one has the right to tell you how to dress or act; however, from a marketing standpoint, appearing or acting certain ways may diminish your overall effectiveness. Since most readers wish to display a highly professional, somewhat conservative, polished image, the following items must be addressed:

1. *Wardrobe*. Read a current issue of one of the magazines catering to image. Consider hiring a wardrobe consultant. In major cities you can find such individuals in the phone book under fashion consultant, image consultant, or wardrobe consultant. While the range of services may differ, most of these consultants will visit your home, examine your wardrobe, and make specific suggestions to help you accomplish your image-related goals. Some consultants will even take you shopping or go shopping for you for a fee.

2. *Logo, stationery*. These must be tastefully designed and consistently applied to all of the firm's printed material.

3. *Association membership*. Successful professionals join and display the emblems of their industry associations (see the section on atmospherics, to follow).

4. *Community relations*. Become involved with community, civic, and professional groups (see Chapter 21, on leveraging your memberships).

5. *Your receptionist*. This person must have a pleasant, commanding speaking voice and know how to properly convey the firm's desired image.

This list is by no means comprehensive but is presented to stimulate your awareness of image-related factors. Throughout this book, keep in mind that your image and your firm's image, whether clearly spelled out or heretofore unknown or unrecognized, will color the perception of your clients and targets with virtually the same impact as your verbal or written message. Use Figure 25–2 to assess your image.

If you want to convey the image of being a high-quality professional, operating a high-quality professional service firm, then "think, feel, and act quality," within your relationships, certainly regarding your appearance, in the services you provide, and the resources you employ. And, as one consultant noted, image is really nothing more than creating assumptions in others. Psychologists have long known that people have been very much influenced by looks and that most of us conclude that what looks good must be good.

It is difficult to maintain a false image consistently or one that is beyond your area of personal comfort. If you seek to change your image, recognize that the process will take some time. As Earl Nightingale says, initially you'll have to "act the part." Eventually, you can embrace and maintain the image that you desire.

A key component in maintaining an effective, highly professional image is simply to like yourself. We live in an era in which a preponderance of working adults are not happy with their appearance. Reputable pollsters and survey researchers have found that most men want to be a bit taller, have more hair, have at least one different facial feature, be more muscular, and have better posture.

Most women are unhappy with their hair and hair color, believe that they weigh too much, believe their figures are unsatisfactory, wish to be taller, and have at least a dozen other image quests. Psychologists, therapists, and counselors contend that being happy with yourself and being basically happy with the way you look does more for the image you project than nearly anything else. Obviously your wardrobe and other professional accoutrements play a big role in your overall image, and combined with liking yourself, provide a good base from which you can become effective at personal selling.

ATMOSPHERICS

Your clients and office visitors are exposed to elements of your image when visiting your office. Your office's atmospherics—that is your personal image as reflected in your office—speak loudly.

For example, the types of magazines you display reveal something

FIGURE 25–2
Assessing Your Image

Wardrobe	
Suits	Blue, gray, and beige are best, 100% wool or a wool/polyester blend. Solids, subtle plaids, tweeds, pinstripes. Ladies—brown, camel, maroon, and black colors also okay.
Shirts	White, light blue; and blue, maroon, beige, or brown pinstripe on white. Ladies—much greater color assortment.
Ties	Silk, or polyester that looks like silk, cotton, or wool. Avoid any odd or garishly colored or designed tie.
Shoes	Black, brown, cordovan. Slip on, lace, wing-tips. Ladies—add gray and blue.
Socks	Dark colors, over the calf. Ladies—flesh-colored pantyhose.
Belts	Black or brown, avoid fancy buckles. Ladies—in vogue with season.
Coat	Blue, camel. Ladies—add gray, not too dressy.
Attache case	Dark brown or cordovan.
Glasses	Nontinted with dark rims.
Jewelry	Thin, gold, never loud or brassy.
Personal	
Grooming	Short hairstyle, neatly trimmed beard or moustache. Sideburns according to latest trend. Fingernails—clean, short. Ladies—moderate length hairstyle; fingernails—professionally manicured in appearance.
Accessories	Pens—silver or gold Cross. Pipe, cigar, cigarettes (avoid if possible).
Automobile	
	Late model, noncompact car, clean, dent free. Noncluttered and in top operating condition.

about your firm. If *National Geographic, Scientific American,* or *Psychology Today* or some type of international magazine is displayed, you convey a "global," intellectual, perhaps philosophical approach to business and the image that certain coveted achievements and milestones have perhaps already been reached. If *Forbes, Fortune,* and similar publications are displayed, visitors perceive a fair degree of success and an image of at least a moderate level of sophistication. If you display *Time, Newsweek, Business Week, Der Spiegel,* or *US News and World Report,* the background or interest of the firm is not necessarily reflected. If *Life, Le Monde, People, Match,* or *Sports*

Wardrobe

Suits   _____

_____

_____

Shirts   _____

_____

Ties   _____

_____

Shoes   _____

_____

Socks   _____

Belts   _____

_____

Coat   _____

Attache case _____

Glasses   _____

Jewelry   _____

Personal

Grooming _____

_____

_____

_____

Accessories _____

_____

Automobile

_____

_____

Illustrated are displayed, it's more than likely for the reading enjoyment of the visitors but may not convey the image you desire.

One Los Angeles-based design consultant observed that all too often "office decorations are approached as an afterthought," as sort of a routine personalizing, something that is done after consulting a catalog from an office furniture manufacturer. Yet your office, and the offices of your firm, help to express a unique style and personality.

Act objectively, fill out the chart in Figure 25–3 to assess your office atmospherics. If you suspect there is room for improvement, much like you

FIGURE 25–3
Assessing Your Atmospherics

Building

Exterior

Appearance *OK - Older building in downtown area*

Outdoor sign *Not Applicable*

Parking *Very difficult*

Neighborhood *Appropriate*

Lobby

Decor *Fair - needs modernization*

Signage *OK - white lettering on black template*

Cleanliness *Clean, but with poor lighting looks worse*

Offices

Interior—Reception Area

Decor *OK - could use new drapes and fixtures*

Layout *A little cramped*

Screening *Good - other offices are not visible*

Displays *Good - association plaques, our brochure, &*
Fortune Magazine

Interior—Offices, Hallway

Cleanliness *Good*

Illumination *Good but fixtures are old*

Decor *Fair*

Density *Hallways are not wide, offices are OK*

Staff

Professional Staff

Dress *Excellent - pin stripes, conservative, fashionable*

Demeanor *Professional at all times*

Other *Appear active, busy*

Support Staff (i.e., Receptionist)

Dress *Excellent*

Demeanor *Perhaps too young to convey desired image*

Attentiveness *OK*

Building

Exterior

   Appearance _____

   Outdoor sign _____

   Parking _____

   Neighborhood _____

Lobby

   Decor _____

   Signage _____

   Cleanliness _____

Offices

Interior—Reception Area

   Decor _____

   Layout _____

   Screening _____

   Displays _____

Interior—Offices, Hallway

   Cleanliness _____

   Illumination _____

   Decor _____

   Density _____

Staff

Professional Staff

   Dress _____

   Demeanor _____

   Other _____

Support Staff (i.e., Receptionist)

   Dress _____

   Demeanor _____

   Attentiveness _____

would in choosing an advertising agency, go about the process of choosing an office decorating consultant.

SHOW US YOUR PLAQUES

As a parting note, be sure to display any trade association plaques or membership certificates. Older, more established professional service firms usually belong to at least one trade association and display the plaque proudly. The plaque often indicates the year you joined, which delivers a message to visitors.

It is probably best to shield your offices from the reception area. Firms that have high regard for their employees and are trying to convey a sophisticated image shield employees from view.

It is acceptable and, in fact, recommended to display company literature. Visitors often read any brochures that are available, and if they can't read them before speaking to you, they read them afterwards.

Now, in Part Six, we turn to managing marketing functions.

PART SIX

Managing Your Marketing Functions

We designed this book with the goal of having it be a practical marketing blueprint for you, the service provider. This section examines the strategic aspects of marketing and concludes with a step-by-step examination of the procedures involved in preparing your personal marketing plan. The step-by-step techniques presented in this section have worked for thousands of professional service firms over the past 25 years.

CHAPTER 26

Developing Your Strategic Plan

By now you know well that the client-centered firm adapts its services, promotional strategies, and personal selling approaches to the needs and buying practices of its targets of opportunity. The tool for accomplishing this is the strategic plan.

In this chapter you will learn how to:

☐ Define your firm's mission.

☐ Define your purpose.

☐ Articulate the values that underlie your marketing and client service activities.

☐ Make strategic business unit (SBU) decisions.

☐ Allocate your time and resources to appropriate growth strategies.

DEFINING YOUR FIRM'S MISSION

A mission statement consists of answers to the following question: "We exist as a firm to do or provide what, for whom, using what technology?"

Here is a mission statement of one successful management consultant: "We are a professional service firm providing written and oral advice and training to clients in the accounting and consulting professions using computer-assisted technology when it delivers value-added results."

DEFINING YOUR FIRM'S PURPOSE

Your purpose statement defines your firm's service commitment to its clients. This is an external focus that spells out what the firm specifically commits to provide to its clients.

Here is an example: "We provide practical solutions in a manner that empowers the client's staff, and produces results far greater than the costs to the client in obtaining the services."

ARTICULATING THE VALUES
THAT DRIVE YOUR FIRM

Values refer to the conditions that must be present as you conduct your marketing and client service functions. One of Dick's clients listed the following values:

- Integrity in everything attempted and accomplished
- State-of-the-art technology—it's enhanced or dropped
- Client-centered services—promotion and relationship building
- Strategic focus to avoid dissonant activities
- Conversion of normative theory into practical choices and actions

MAKING STRATEGIC BUSINESS
UNIT DECISIONS

A strategic business unit refers to the major functional areas of your current practice and the amount of *additional* resources you will devote to each. You can make three decisions: maintain, build, or withdraw resources.

An accounting firm client prepared this table:

Business	Maintain	Build	Withdraw
a. Audit	X		
b. Tax		40%	
c. Management advisory services		60%	

In this example, it was decided to maintain the current level of resources in the audit side of the practice, while investing additional resources in building both the tax and management advisory services functions. No function was to have resources withdrawn from it at this time. The table is simple to prepare but it requires extensive analysis before making allocation decisions. This process is beyond the scope of this book.

BUILDING YOUR MIX OF GROWTH STRATEGIES

There are four different strategies for achieving growth: penetration, innovation, expansion, and, in today's rapidly changing environment, retention of one's clients and markets.

1. *Penetration* focuses on increasing sales of current services to existing industry-market niches. This takes several forms.

   a. Sell extensions or add-ons to current engagements

   b. Sell other services to clients

   c. Attract new clients within the current niches

2. *Expansion* concentrates on selling current services to prospects and clients in *new* industry-market niches.

3. *Innovation* focuses on developing and marketing *new services* to targets within both existing niches and new target niches.

4. *Retention* stresses continuation of services to desirable clients you can't afford to lose. Remember that a client saved is a client earned.

The current mix of growth strategies for Dick's practice and for Jeff's practice is presented on the next page.

You can include more factors in your strategic plan, but the ones discussed and demonstrated in this chapter have been proven to be useful to the busy professional.

Growth Strategies for Dick Connor, CMC

a.	Penetration	60%
b.	Innovation	20%
c.	Expansion	0%
d.	Retention	20%

Growth Strategies for Jeff Davidson, CMC

a.	Penetration	30%
b.	Innovation	30%
c.	Expansion	20%
d.	Retention	20%

Appendix D contains a copy of Dick's current strategic plan. We suggest that you study it and prepare your own. Appendix C, "Developing a Strategic Focus," is included for additional background.

We complete the book with a discussion of how to prepare your personal marketing plan.

CHAPTER 27

Preparing Your Marketing Plan

You have now been thoroughly immersed in the client-centered marketing approach for the marketing of your professional and consulting services.

It's now time to organize and coordinate those activities that will develop and enhance your relationship with those people who will be interested in using, retaining, or referring your firm and your services. This is most efficiently done by preparing a marketing plan. The charts and worksheets used throughout the book, added to your research efforts and scheduling of client-centered marketing activities, comprise a sound marketing plan.

This chapter assists you in preparing your marketing plan and also provides answers to the following questions:

☐ What are the components of a client-centered marketing plan?

☐ Must some marketing-related thinking occur each day?

☐ Will an effectively implemented client-centered marketing plan work for you?

A CLIENT-CENTERED MARKETING PLAN

A client-centered marketing plan for a professional service firm consists of five components:

FIGURE 27–1
Information to Complete Your Personal Marketing Plan

PERSONAL MARKETING PLAN

For:_____

From: ____/ ____/ ____ to ____/ ____/ ____
(Current Planning-Action Period)

1. Targets of Opportunity
   a. "A" and "B" clients to be contacted this period
   b. "C" clients with potential for upgrading
   c. Prospective clients to be contacted

2. Targets of Attention
   a. "A" and "B" clients with warning signals
   b. "C" and "D" clients with warning signals
   c. Referral sources with a low quality of relationship
   d. "A" and "B" clients with potential for becoming referral sources
   e. Niches requiring attention

3. Targets of Influence
   a. Potential nonclient influentials to be contacted

4. Promotion
   a. Promotional actions to be taken this period

5. Prospecting
   a. Prospecting actions to be taken this period

6. Other Marketing Actions
   a. Services to be enhanced or developed
   b. Marketing information systems to be developed
   c. Self-development actions to be taken this period

---

1. Assessing one's practice and markets to identify opportunities and problems

2. Establishing priorities

3. Setting goals to be accomplished during the marketing planning period

4. Allocating and organizing the resources required to accomplish the period's goals

5. Scheduling, applying, and monitoring results

The end product or "hard-copy" is the marketing plan. Market planning converts your intentions into commitment and your insights into action. *You must put your plan in writing*.

On completion of a training workshop in setting marketing goals, one firm decided to use their copier to reduce the written plan to pocket size, laminate it, and offer it to staff professionals as a daily memory jogger.

Putting your ideas in writing provides discipline. Hazy thoughts can become precisely formulated strategies when committed to writing. A written plan enables you to measure your progress and to experience a satisfying feeling of accomplishment as you note completion dates for each part of your plan.

We have prepared a personal marketing plan form that incorporates every figure and recommended marketing step discussed in the book. Figure 27–1 can be used as a reference in completing Figure 27–2, "Personal Marketing Plan."

SELECT LITTLE GOALS TO WIN EARLY AND OFTEN

During your initial planning sessions, select goals that can be worked on in a piecemeal basis. For example, "Prepare spreadsheet for completing Figure 3–2" would be listed in Section 6 of your plan outline.

To aid in initiating the marketing planning process, we provide sample goals statements in Figure 27–3, a sample financial goals statement in Figure 27–4, and a refresher list of client-centered activities in Figure 27–5.

Build in follow-up. When you set an accomplishment date for a goal, note this in your pocket calendar and desk calendar as a reminder. If you constantly miss goals, determine why. Remember, results accrue over a period of time.

The client-centered marketing approach has proved successful for professional service firms, from some of the very largest to one-person firms. If you effectively implement your client-centered marketing plan, it will work for you. Thanks for reading all the way through.

FIGURE 27–2
Sample Form for Your Personal Marketing Plan

PERSONAL MARKETING PLAN

For:_____

From__/__/__ to__/__/__

1. **Targets of Opportunity**

	Who?	What?	When?
a.	_____	_____	_____
b.	_____	_____	_____
c.	_____	_____	_____
d.	_____	_____	_____
e.	_____	_____	_____

2. **Targets of Attention**

	Who?	What?	When?
a.	_____	_____	_____
b.	_____	_____	_____
c.	_____	_____	_____
d.	_____	_____	_____
e.	_____	_____	_____

3. **Targets of Influence**

	Who?	What?	When?
a.	_____	_____	_____
b.	_____	_____	_____
c.	_____	_____	_____
d.	_____	_____	_____
e.	_____	_____	_____

4. Promotion

	What?	Where?	When?
a.	_____	_____	_____
b.	_____	_____	_____
c.	_____	_____	_____
d.	_____	_____	_____
e.	_____	_____	_____

5. Prospecting

	What?	Where?	When?
a.	_____	_____	_____
b.	_____	_____	_____
c.	_____	_____	_____
d.	_____	_____	_____
e.	_____	_____	_____

6. Other Marketing Actions

	What?	Where?	When?
a.	_____	_____	_____
b.	_____	_____	_____
c.	_____	_____	_____
d.	_____	_____	_____
e.	_____	_____	_____

FIGURE 27–3
Sample Goals Statements

Performance

Financial
Increase average chargeable hour rate from $___ to $___ by __/__/__.
Bill _____ hours in month of ____.
Identify delinquent accounts by __/__/__.

Existing Clients
Identify causes of lost clients by __/__/__.
Contact _____ at _____ to discuss _____ by __/__/__.

Existing Markets
Identify existing markets by __/__/__.
Select one market to estimate potential for growth by __/__/__.

Existing Services
Assess client-centeredness of _____ by __/__/__.
                                    (service)

Assess payoff from specialization in _____ by __/__/__.
                                            (industry)

Referrals

Assess the quality of relationship with _____ by __/__/__.
                                              (who)

Select one referral to "educate" about _____ by __/__/__.
                                              (what)

Targets

Select one prospective client in potential new business pipeline for follow-up
    sales contact by __/__/__.
Identify desirable potential clients in industry _____ by __/__/__.

Promotion

Establish promotion objectives by __/__/__.
Schedule entertainment with _____ by __/__/__.
                                    (client)

Other

Attend _____ on __/__/__.
              (program)
Read _____ by __/__/__.
            (publication)

FIGURE 27–4
Financial Goals Statement

For:_____, to (____/____/____)

My financial goals for this period are: _____
_____
_____
_____
_____

I intend to increase my personal billing revenue from _____ to
$_____, an increase of ___%. (most recent 12 months)

I intend to increase the number of personal chargeable hours from ____ to ____,
an increase/decrease of ___%.

I want/intend to increase my average *hourly rate* from $____ to $____.

My key goal to accomplish in this period is: _____
_____
_____
_____
_____
_____

During this planning period I also intend to accomplish the following: _____
_____
_____
_____
_____
_____

The problems I anticipate, if any, in achieving these goals are: _____
_____
_____
_____
_____
_____

The resources I can draw on to help me overcome these problems include:
_____
_____
_____
_____
_____

FIGURE 27–5
Refresher List of Client-Centered Marketing Activities

Existing Key Clients

Retention planning for _____

_____

Expanding services for _____

_____

Referral development with _____

_____

Existing Marginal Clients

Upgrade service and financial relationships with _____

_____

Terminate or transfer _____

_____

Other Existing Client Actions

Corrective actions to remove causes of lost clients _____

_____

Actions to capitalize on sources of desirable new clients _____

_____

Other _____

_____

Markets and Niches

To research _____

_____

To penetrate _____

_____

To abandon _____

_____

Referral Sources

Improve relationships with _____

_____

Develop additional sources—leverage _____

_____

Contact to educate _____

_____

Glossary

"A" client   a client whom you consider to be of exceptional value to you because of fee volume, prestige, potential for growth, and good chemistry.

Action letter   a letter that enhances the professional-client relationship by displaying a high level of quality.

Advertising copy   the written message portion of a print advertisement or the dialogue of a spoken advertisement.

AIDA process   creating a favorable *awareness* (A), sharing *information* (I) to develop an interest in seeing you, conducting need-driven *discussions* (D), and building a desire to proceed to *action* (A).

Atmosphere   that part of your personal image that is reflected by your office decor, location, staffing, and layout.

"B" client   your bread and butter clients. They pay their bills, but do not represent much potential for good fee growth.

Bulk rate   a reduced rate offered by the U.S. Post Office for mass mailers.

"C" client   those who seek discounts and additional free services and are frequently slow in paying your invoices.

Client-centered marketing   the continuing process of developing and enhancing relationships with clients and other receptive people who are or can be useful to you in using, retaining, and referring you and your services.

Client referral   an existing client's providing you with leads or introductions, or vouching for you.

Comfort zone   the range of effective, self-initiated behavior in an activity area; the area of professional behavior where one is productive, confident, and forthright in one's communications and actions.

Concept paper   a marketing tool for moving the client further along in the selling process and determining if the client has significant interest in pursuing with you a solution to a problem.

"D" client   your troublesome clients; the ones you wish you had not accepted.

Direct mail   a form of advertising in which a business communication is sent to preselected targets.

Direct mail package   a sales communication or request containing five typical elements: the letter, enclosure, reply, reply envelope, and outside envelope.

Existing client   a client you now serve or will serve during the coming period.

Free writing   plunging in and writing your thoughts as fast as you can get them on a page.

Goal   a specific statement of what you expect or intend to accomplish and when.

Hard-sell approach   a marketing approach that focuses on getting known, and places emphasis on "our firm" and "our services" but does not focus on client needs.

Image   the sum total of all the perceptions your clients and all others have about you and your practice.

Industry   all clients, prospective clients, and suspects in your practice area having the same four-digit SIC number.

Leveraging   concentrating on the smallest number of clients, prospects, niches, and targets that will produce the largest amount of profitable revenue; a multiplier of activity that produces a "cascade" effect of results.

List compiler/supplier   a direct mail marketing organization that provides names and addresses of target markets for a fee.

Logo   a symbol or design (used on stationery and literature) that aids others in identifying and remembering you, your firm, or your organization.

Market   the postal ZIP codes in your practice area for a specific SIC; a defined geographical area.

Marketing plan   the "hard-copy" end-product of the marketing planning process.

Marketing planning   the continuing process of: (1) auditing one's practice and markets to identify opportunities and problems, (2) establishing priority, (3) setting goals, (4) allocating and organizing resources required to accomplish the goals, and (5) scheduling, doing, and monitoring results.

NCIs   nonclient influentials, people in the infrastructure who can assist you in meeting your marketing objectives and goals.

New business discussions   the face-to-face meetings with prospective clients to define the existing and desired situations as well as a solution program for delivering the required results.

News release   an announcement of community, state, national, or international interest distributed to print media by the organization for whom the release is written.

Niche   an abbreviated term for the intersection of industry and market.

Personal promotion   first-person activities you undertake to favorably present your capabilities in meeting client needs.

Personal selling   a professional marketing effort involving face-to-face communication and feedback with prospective users of your services.

Potential clients   see **Suspects**.

Press kit   a coordinated set of materials that answers most of the questions an editor or producer would like to know before deciding to interview you.

Press release see **News Release.**

Prewriting the stage where article ideas or topics are hatched, and in which one is exploring manageable angles on which to write.

Promotion the process of informing, persuading, or reminding targets of opportunity and influence about your firm's ability to meet client needs. Also involves stimulating inquiries and managing your image.

Proposal a document that is designed to describe the firm's ability to perform a specific task (or tasks). Indicates that the firm has the facilities, human resources, management experience, and track record to assure successful project performance and completion.

Prospect a former suspect who has agreed to meet with you to discuss a need situation and has not yet purchased your proposed solution program.

Prospecting the activities involved in obtaining appointments with qualified suspects for the purpose of converting them into clients or prospects.

Public relations all planned activities that you undertake to influence public opinion about you and your firm.

Publicity a key component of public relations; involves media coverage of events including background information, descriptions, relevant data, or other current information involving you, your service, and your firm or organization.

Readership (or audience) profile descriptive information and facts about subscribers (or audience) of media sources.

Referrals clients and nonclients who mention your name to others and provide you with introductions and leads to new business opportunities.

Reputation the perception of value and integrity that you've demonstrated in serving your clients and community.

RFP a request for proposal is a solicitation made by a government or private agency that is seeking the services of an outside contractor to perform a specific task or tasks.

Standard Industrial Classification (SIC) a 4-digit number assigned by the U.S. Department of Commerce to identify commercial entities.

Strategic focus selecting whom one will serve and in what ways, then developing and promoting services that fill unmet or poorly met needs of clients and prospective clients.

Strategic thinker in the context of marketing professional services one who develops a client-centered orientation, identifies strengths and matches them with present potential market opportunities, and focuses on profitability, not necessarily volume. The strategic thinker puts the status quo on trial and asks pointed questions.

Suspects desirable nonclient organizations possessing suspected opportunity who have not yet agreed to move with you.

Targets of influence nonclient referral sources who, while not likely to use your services, may favorably influence others to do so.

Targets of opportunity organizations, firms, and individuals that may have need for your services and who represent service/revenue opportunities for your firm.

Testimonials a written recommendation or expression of appreciation written by a third party (client).

Traditional approach a marketing approach that is reactive and deals with existing client problems as they arise, but provides little overall strategy or coordination of marketing effort.

Unsolicited proposal a proposal written in response to a perceived or known need and not in response to an RFP.

APPENDIX A

Standard Industrial Classification (SIC) Categories

Industry	SIC no.
Agriculture Production-Crops	100
Agriculture Produc-Livestock	200
Drilling Oil & Gas Wells	1381
Oil & Gas Field Exploration	1382
Oil & Gas Field Services NEC	1389
Misc Nonmetallic Minerals	1499
Operative Builders	1531
Gen Bldg Contractors Nonres	1540
Construction-Not Bldg Constr	1600
Construction-Spl Contractors	1700
Food & Kindred Products	2000
Meat Products	2010
Dairy Products	2020
Canned-Preserved Fruits-Vegs	2030
Flour & Other Grain Mill Pds	2041
Wet Corn Milling	2046
Prepared Feeds for Animals	2048
Bakery Products	2050

Industry	SIC no.
Beet Sugar	2063
Candy & Other Confectionery	2065
Malt Beverages	2082
Distilled Rectif Blend Bevrg	2085
Bottled-Canned Soft Drinks	2086
Food Preparation NEC	2099
Textile Mill Products	2200
Knitting Mills	2250
Floor Covering Mills	2270
Lumber & Wood Products	2400
Wood Buildings-Mobile Homes	2450
Household Furniture	2510
Office Furniture	2520
Paper & Allied Products	2600
Convert Paper-Paperbd Pd NEC	2649
Printing Publishing & Allied	2700
Newspapers: Publishing-Print	2711
Periodicals: Publishing-Print	2721
Books: Publishing & Printing	2731

213

Industry	SIC no.	Industry	SIC no.
Commercial Printing	2750	Ordnance & Accessories	3480
Manifold Business Forms	2761	Valves & Pipe Fittings Ex Bras	3494
Greeting Card Publishing	2771	Fabricated Metal Prds NEC	3499
Chemicals & Allied Prods	2800	Engines & Turbines	3510
Indl Inorganic Chemicals	2810	Farm & Garden Machinery & Eq	3520
Plastic Matr Synthetic Resin	2820	Construction Machinery & Eqp	3531
Drugs	2830	Oil Field Machinery & Equip	3533
Biological Products	2831	Hoist-Indus Cranes-Monorail	3536
Medicinal Chemical Biotanical Pds	2833	Indl Trucks-Tractors-Trailers	3537
Pharmaceutical Preparations	2834	Metalworking Industry & Eqp.	3540
Soap & Other Detergents	2841	Special Industry Machinery	3550
Paints-Varnishes-Lacquers	2850	Pollution Control Machinery	3558
Industrial Organic Chemicals	2860	General Industrial Mach & Eq	3560
Agriculture Chemicals	2870	Office Computing & Acctg Mch	3570
Misc Chemical Products	2890	Refrig & Service Ind Machine	3580
Petroleum Refining	2911	Elec & Electr Mach Eq & Supp	3600
Paving & Roofing Materials	2950	Elec Transmission & Distr Eq	3610
Rubber & Misc Plastics Prods	3000	Electrical Industrial Appar	3620
Fabricated Rubber Prods NEC	3069		
Misc Plastic Products	3079	Industrial Controls	3622
		Electrical Lighting-Wiring Eq	3640
Flat Glass	3210	Tele & Telegraph Apparatus	3661
Glass Containers	3221	Radio TV Transmttng Equipment	3662
Cement Hydraulic	3241	Electronic Components & Access	3670
Structural Clay Products	3250		
Pottery Products NEC	3269	Semiconductors & Rel Devices	3674
		Electronic Components NEC	3679
Concrete Gypsum & Plaster	3270	Electronic Computing Equip	3680
Abrasive Asbestos & Misc Min	3290	Computers-Mini & Micro	3681
Blast Furnaces & Steel Works	3310	Computers-Mainframe	3682
Prim Smelt-Refin Nonfer Mtl	3330		
Rolling & Draw Nonfer Metal	3350	Computer Terminals	3683
		Computer Disk & Tape Drives	3684
Misc Primary Metal Products	3390	Optical Char-Laser Scanners	3685
Metal Cans & Shipping Cont	3410	Computer Graphics Systems	3686
Hardware NEC	3429	Office Automation Systems	3687
Heating Equip & Plumbing Fix	3430	Computer Peripherals	3688
Solar Energy Equip & Comp	3437	Computer Equpment NEC	3689
		X-ray, Electromedical Apparat	3693
Mtl Doors-Frames-Mold & Trim	3442	Robotics	3695
Fabricated Plate Work	3443	Electrical Machy & Equip NEC	3699
Sheet Metal Work	3444	Motor Vehicles & Car Bodies	3711
Prefab Metal Bldgs & Comp	3448	Motor Vehicle Parts-Accessor	3714
Misc Metal Work	3449		
		Motor Homes	3716
Bolts-Nuts-Screws-Riv-Washrs	3452	Aircraft & Parts	3720
Metal Forgings & Stampings	3460		

Industry	SIC no.	Industry	SIC no.
Aircraft	3721	Whsl-Metals & Minerals	5050
Aircraft Parts & Aux Equip	3728	Whsl-Elec Apparatus & Equip	5063
Ship-Boat Building & Repairing	3730		
		Whsl-Elec Applicance TV & Radio	5064
Motorcycles Bicycles & Parts	3750	Whsl-Electronic Parts & Equip	5065
Travel Trailers & Campers	3792	Whsl-Hardwr Plum Heat Equip	5070
Engr Lab & Research Equip	3811	Whsl-Machinery & Equipment	5080
Measuring & Controlling Inst	3820	Whsl-Durable Goods NEC	5099
Automatic Cntls Envri & Appl.	3822		
		Whsl-Drugs & Proprietary	5120
Industrial Measurement Instr	3823	Whsl-Groceries & Related Pds	5140
Elec Meas & Test Instr	3825	Whsl-Petroleum & Petro Pds	5170
Meas & Controlling Dev NEC	3829	Whsl-Nondurable Goods NEC	5199
Optical Instruments & Lenses	3830	Retail-Lumber & Bldg Mat	5211
Surg & Med Instruments & App	3841		
		Retail-Mobile Home Dealers	5270
Ortho-Prosth-Surg Appl & Supp	3842	Retail-Department Stores	5311
Dental Equip & Supplies	3843	Retail-Variety Stores	5331
Opthalmic Goods	3851	Retail-Grocery Stores	5411
Photographic Equip & Suppl	3861	Retail-Auto Dealers & Gas Stat	5500
Watches Clocks & Parts	3870		
		Retail-Apparel & Acces Store	5600
Jewelry-Precious Metals	3911	Retail-Computer Stores	5995
Silverware-Plateware	3914	Retail-Stores NEC	5999
Musical Instruments	3931	Savings & Loan Associations	6120
Toys & Amusement Sport Goods	3940	Personal Credit Institutions	6140
Pens-Pencil & Oth Office Mat	3950		
		Business Credit Institutions	6150
Misc Manufacturing Industries	3990	Finance-Services	6199
Railroads-Line Haul Operating	4011	Security & Commodity Brokers	6200
Intercity & Rural Hywy Trans	4131	Insurance Agents Brokers	6400
Trucking-Local & Long Distance	4210	Real Estate	6500
Water Transportation	4400		
		Operators-Nonres Bldgs	6512
Air Transportation-Certified	4511	Operators-Apartment Bldgs	6513
Transportation Services	4700	Real Estate Agents & Mgrs	6531
Telephone Communication	4811	Real Estate Dealers	6532
Telegraph Communication	4821	Subdivid Develop Ex Cemetery	6552
Radio-TV Broadcasters	4830		
		Oil Royalty Traders	6792
Communications Services NEC	4890	Patent Owners & Lessors	6794
Cable Television Operators	4891	Real Estate Investment Trust	6798
Telephone Interconnect Sys.	4892	Hotel-Motels	7011
Natural Gas Transmis-Distr	4923	Serv-Personal	7200
Sanitary Serv	4950		
		Serv-Advertising Agencies	7311
Whsl-Autos & Parts	5012	Credit Reporting Agencies	7321
Whsl-Lumber & Constr Matl	5030	Serv-Clean & Maint to Bldg NEC	7349
Whsl-Sporting & Recrea Goods	5040		

Industry	SIC no.	Industry	SIC no.
Personnel Supply Services	7360	Commercial Testing Labs	7397
Serv-Computer & Data Process	7370	Serv-Business Services NEC	7399
		Serv-Automotive Repair & Ser	7500
Serv-CMP Program & Software	7372	Serv-Motion Picture Productn	7810
Serv-Data Processing Svcs	7374	Serv-Misc Amusement & Recrea	7990
Serv-Computer Rel Svcs NEC	7379	Serv-Nursing-Person Care Fac	8050
Serv-Resrch & Devlpmnt Lab	7391	Serv-Hospitals	8060
Serv-Mgmt Consulting & PR	7392	Medical & Dental Labs	8070
		Outpatient Care Facilities	8081
Serv-Detective & Protective	7393	Health & Allied Services NEC	8091
Serv-Equip Rental & Leasing	7394	Serv-Educational	8200
Photofinishing Laboratories	7395	Serv-Engineering & Architect	8911

A Sampling of Industry, Professional, Small Business, and Trade Associations

ADMINISTRATION, MANAGEMENT

American Management Association
135 West 50th Street
New York, NY 10020
(212) 586–8100

American Society for Public
  Administration
1120 G Street, NW, Suite 500
Washington, DC 20005
(202) 393–7878

American Society of Association
  Executives
1575 Eye Street, NW
Washington, DC 20005
(202) 626–2723

Data Processing Management
  Association
505 Busse Highway
Park Ridge, IL 60068
(312) 693–5070

National Management Association
2210 Arbor Boulevard
Dayton, OH 45439
(513) 294–0421

Sales & Marketing Executives,
  International
Statler Office Tower, Suite 458
Cleveland, OH 44115
(216)771–6650

COMMUNICATIONS, GRAPHICS, AND PRINTING

American Association of
  Advertising Agencies
666 Third Avenue
New York, NY 10017
(212) 682–2500

Direct Marketing Association
6 East 43rd Street
New York, NY 10017
(212) 689–4977

International Association of
Business Communicators
870 Market Street, Suite 940
San Francisco, CA 94102
(415) 433–3400

Printing Industries of America
1730 North Lynn Street
Arlington, VA 22209
(703) 841–8100

Professional Photographers of
America, Inc.
1090 Executive Way
Des Plaines, IL 60018
(312) 299–8161

Public Relations Society of
America
33 Irving Place
New York, NY 10003
(212) 995–2230

CONSTRUCTION, CONTRACTING

Air Conditioning Contractors of
America
1513 16th St., N.W.
Washington, DC 20036
(202) 483–9370

Associated Builders & Contractors,
Inc.
729 15th Street, NW
Washington, DC 20005
(202) 637–8800

Associated General Contractors of
America
1957 E Street, NW
Washington, DC 20006
(202) 393-2040

National Association of Home
Builders
15th and M Streets, NW
Washington, DC 20005
(202) 822–0200

National Electrical Contractors
Association
7315 Wisconsin Avenue, 13th
Floor
Bethesda, MD 20814
(301) 657–3110

Painting and Decorating
Contractors
3913 Old Lee Hwy., Suite 33B
Fairfax, VA 22030
(703) 359–0826

FINANCIAL, REAL ESTATE

American Bankers Association
1120 Connecticut Avenue, NW
Washington, DC 20036
(202) 663–5011

American Institute of Real Estate
Appraisers
430 North Michigan Avenue
Chicago, IL 60611
(312) 329–8559

American Society of Appraisers
535 Herndon Pkwy.
Herndon, VA 22070
(703) 478–2228

American Society of Professional
Estimators
6911 Richmond Hwy., Suite 230
Alexandria, VA 22306
(703) 765–2700

Building Owners and Managers
Association International
1250 Eye St., NW
Washington, DC 20005
(202) 289–7000

Financial Executives Institute
10 Madison Avenue
P.O. Box 1938
Morristown, NJ 07960
(201) 898–4600

Independent Insurance Agents of
America, Inc.
100 Church Street
New York, NY 10007
(212) 285–4250

Institute of Certified Financial
Planners
Two Denver Highlands
10065 E. Harvard Ave., Suite 320
Denver, CO 80231
(303) 751-7600

Mortgage Bankers Association of
America
1125 15th Street, NW
Washington, DC 20005
(202) 861–6500

Million Dollar Round Table
2340 River Road
Des Plaines, IL 60018
(312) 298–1120

National Association of Bank
Women
500 North Michigan Avenue, Suite
1400
Chicago, IL 60611
(312) 298–1120

National Association of
Professional Insurance Agents
400 North Washington Street
Alexandria, VA 22314
(703) 836–9340

National Association of Realtors
430 North Michigan Avenue
Chicago, IL 60611
(312) 329–8200

Security Traders Association
One World Trade Center
New York, NY 10048
(212) 524–0484

Securities Industry Association
2800 28th St., Suite 101
Santa Monica, CA 90405
(213) 450–4141

Society of Real Estate Appraisers
225 North Michigan Avenue
Chicago, IL 60601
(312) 819–2400

INTERNATIONAL

World Association of Women
Entrepreneurs
corso Europa 14
I–20122 Milan, Italy

Intl. Association of State Trading
Organizations of Developing
Countries
Titova 104
Postanski Fah 92
Yu–61000 Ljubljana, Yugoslavia

Foreign Trade Association
Weyerstrasse 2
D–5000 Cologne 1, Federal
Republic of Germany

International Trade Center
Palais des Nations
CH–1211 Geneva 10, Switzerland

Enterprise Development
  Association
High Orchard
125 Markyate Road
Dagenham, Essex Rm 8 ZLB
  England

International Association of Crafts
  & Small and Medium Sized
  Enterprises
Schwarztorstrasse 26
Case Postale 2721
CH–3001 Bern, Switzerland

Career Women's Forum
Case Postale 39
CH–1211 Geneva 12, Switzerland

LEISURE, TOURISM, AND TRAVEL

American Hotel and Motel
  Association
1201 New York Ave., NW
Washington, DC 20005
(202) 289–3100

American Society of Travel Agents
1101 King St., Suite 200
Alexandria, VA 22314
(703) 739–2782

National Recreation and Park
  Association
3101 Park Center Drive
Alexandria, VA 22302
(703) 820–4940

Travel Industry Association of
  America
1133 21st St., N.W.
2 Lafayette Center
Washington, DC 20036
(202) 293–1433

MANUFACTURING

American Association of Meat
  Processors
224 East High Street, P.O. Box
  269
Elizabethtown, PA 17022
(717) 367–1168

American Textile Manufacturers
  Institute
1801 K St., NW, Suite 900
Washington, DC 20006
(202) 862–0500

Chemical Manufacturers
  Association
2501 M Street, NW
Washington, DC 20037
(202) 887–1100

Farm Equipment Manufacturers
  Association
243 N. Lindbergh Blvd.
St. Louis, MO 63141
(314) 991–0702

Industrial Fabrics Association
  International
345 Cedar Building, Suite 450
St. Paul, MN 55101
(612) 222–2508

National Association of
  Manufacturers
1331 Pennsylvania Ave., NW
Suite 1500 North
Washington, DC 20004
(202) 637–3000

PROFESSIONAL

American Bar Association
750 N. Lake Shore Drive
Chicago, IL 60611
(312) 988–5000

American Institute of Certified
  Public Accountants
1211 Avenue of the Americas
New York, NY 10036
(212) 575–6200

American Institute of Architects
1735 New York Avenue, NW
Washington, DC 20006
(202) 626–7300

American Society of Women
  Accountants
35 East Wacker Drive
Chicago, IL 60601
(312) 726–9030

Independent Computer Consultants
933 Gardenview Office Parkway
St. Louis, MO 63141
(314) 997–4633

Institute of Management
  Consultants
230 Park Avenue, #544
New York, NY 10169
(212) 697–8262

Association of Management
  Consultants
230 Park Avenue, #544
New York, NY 10169
(212) 697–9693

National Association of
  Accountants
10 Paragon Drive
Montvale, NJ 07645
(201) 573–9000

National Society of Public
  Accountants
1010 North Fairfax Street
Alexandria, VA 22314
(703) 549–6400

Professional Engineers in Private
  Practice
1420 King Street
Alexandria, VA 22314
(703) 684–2862

SMALL BUSINESS

American Business Women's
  Association
P.O. Box 8728
9100 Ward Parkway
Kansas City, MO 64114
(816) 361–6621

American Chamber of Commerce
  Executives
4232 King Street
Alexandria, VA 22302
(703) 998–0072

American Federation of Small
  Business
407 South Dearborn Street
Chicago, IL 60605
(312) 427–0206

American Association of Small
  Research Companies
c/o N. Ventures Corp.
222 Third Street
Suite 3150
Cambridge, MA 02142
(617) 491–7906

International Council for Small
  Business
St. Louis University
3674 Lindell Boulevard
St. Louis, MO 63108
(314) 658–3826

National Business League
4324 Georgia Avenue, NW
Washington,DC 20011
(202) 829–5900

National Federation of Independent
  Business
600 Maryland Avenue, S.W.,
  Suite 700
Washington, DC 20024
(202) 554–9000

RETAILING

American Booksellers Association
137 W. 25th St.
New York, NY 10001
(212) 463–8450

American Retail Federation
1616 H Street, NW
Washington, DC 20006
(202) 783–7971

Food Marketing Institute
1750 K Street, NW, Suite 700
Washington, DC 20006
(202) 452–8444

Jewelers of America, Inc.
1271 Avenue of the Americas
Suite 650
New York, NY 10020
(212) 489–0023

National Association of Chain
  Drug Stores
PO Box 1417-D49
Alexandria, VA 22313
(703) 549–3001

National Association of
  Convenience Stores, Inc.
1605 King Street
Alexandria, VA 22314
(703) 684–3600

National Home Furnishing
  Association
P.O. Box 2396
High Point, NC 27261
(312) 595–0200

National Independent Automobile
  Dealers Association
600 E. Las Colinas Boulevard
Suite 314
Irving, TX 75039
(214) 556–0044

National Restaurant Association
1200 17th Street, N.W.
Washington, DC 20036
(202) 331–5900

National Retail Hardware
  Association
770 North High School Road
Indianapolis, IN 46214
(317) 248–1261

Retail Bakers of America
6525 Belcrest Road, Suite 250
Hyattsville, MD 20782
(301) 277–0990

Shoe Service Institute of America
5024 Campbell Boulevard, Suite R
Baltimore, MD 21236
(301) 661–4400

National Retail Merchants
  Association
100 West 31st Street
New York, NY 10001
(212) 244–8780

WHOLESALING

Durable Goods

Automotive Warehouse
  Distributors Association
9140 Ward Parkway, Suite 200
Kansas City, MO 64114
(816) 444–3500

Farm Equipment Wholesalers
  Association
1927 Keokuk Street
Iowa City, IA 52240
(319) 354–5156

National Association of
  Wholesaler-Distributors
1725 K Street, NW
Washington, DC 20006
(202) 872–0885

National Association of Electrical
  Distributors
28 Cross Street
Norwalk, CT 06851
(203) 846–6800

National Building Material
  Distributors
1417 Lake Cook Road
Suite 130
Deerfield, IL 60015
(312) 945–7201

Linen Trade Association
11 West 42nd Street
New York, NY 10036
(212) 944–2230

National Tire Dealers and
  Retreaders Association, Inc.
1250 Eye Street, NW
Washington, DC 20005
(202) 789–2300

National Wholesale Furniture
  Association
PO Box 2482
Highpoint, NC 27261
(919) 884–1566

Nondurable Goods

Grain Elevator and Processing
  Society
Box 15026, Commerce Station
Minneapolis, MN 55415
(612) 339–4626

National Association of Tobacco
  Distributors
1199 N. Fairfax Street, Suite 701
Alexandria, VA 22314
(703) 683–8336

National Wine Distributors
  Association
10400 Roberts Road
Palos Hills, IL 60465
(312) 598–7070

United Fresh Fruit & Vegetable
  Association
727 N. Washington, St.
Alexandria, VA 22314
(703) 836–3410

PUBLIC POLICY

National Governors Association
Hall of States
444 N. Capitol Street, NW
Suite 250
Washington, DC 20001
(202) 624–5300

National League of Cities
1301 Pennsylvania Avenue, NW
Washington, DC 20004
(202) 626–3000

State Governmental Affairs
  Council
1001 Connecticut Avenue, NW
Suite 800
Washington, DC 20036
(202) 659–7605

U.S. Conference of Mayors
1620 Eye Street, NW
Washington, DC 20006
(202) 293–7330

APPENDIX C

Developing a Strategic Focus

A new era for professional service firms in the United States commenced in January 1982. The U.S. Supreme Court issued a ruling that has had profound impact on the management and marketing of professional services. The court struck down tight restrictions on advertising by lawyers, thereby freeing all the professions "for promotional campaigns more comparable to ordinary business advertising."

STRATEGIC MANAGEMENT OF MARKETING

Strategic actions relate to the nature and direction of a practice. The fundamental strategic action is to decide whom one will serve and in what ways. The survival and prosperity of all but the largest "full-service" firms will, in large measure, depend on finding a niche or niches. The key will be to develop and promote client-centered services that fill the unmet (or poorly met) needs of clients and targeted prospective clients in their niche(s).

PROFILE OF THE STRATEGIC THINKER

The strategic management of marketing and the development of a strategic thought process is, indeed, a challenge for most service professionals because they lack education and experience in this area. Let's profile the strategic thinker by examining the types of questions asked and other factors:

1. The strategic thinker develops a client-centered orientation. The client's needs represent a starting point from which marketing strategy is based. The strategic thinker knows that learning what the client values and expects is fundamental to sustaining a profitable practice. In short, the strategic thinker is client driven.

2. The strategic thinker puts the status quo on trial and asks pointed questions such as: "Where are we now? Where are we going? Where do we wish to be going? What will we look like when we get there?" As simple as these questions may seem, few successful professionals have posed them; however, the answers to these questions are important to the strategic management of the practice.

3. The strategic thinker is able to identify strengths and match them with present and potential market opportunities. As management consultant and renowned author Peter Drucker opines, he "feeds opportunities and starves problems." The strategic manager takes the steps necessary to capitalize on high payoff opportunities. Conversely, sacred cows and unprofitable practice areas must be abandoned without passion.

4. The strategic thinker is able to focus on profitability and not necessarily volume, with the goal of working fewer hours but at an increasingly higher hourly rate. This person is also alert to opportunities to employ greater leverage using junior staff personnel but does not make the mistake of trading "class for mass"—a well-developed base of "high-class," prompt-paying clients is desirable over dealing with the multitudes.

MANAGING YOUR MARKETING STRATEGICALLY

The successful, profitable professional service firm of the 1990s will have identified its niche(s). The nature of existing client relationships and growth potential in the industry, as well as the skills, reputation, and interest of the professional will, of course, play a major role in the identification of the niche(s).

The successful professional must work to develop an insider's reputation with the niche or target market. Clients must feel that the services you provide are uniquely tailored to their needs and that the existence of your practice within a convenient distance represents "provident proximity." The goal in developing an insider's reputation with the niche is to be viewed as "somebody special to some special bodies."

IF NECESSARY, REORGANIZE THE FIRM

The successful professional recognizes the need to organize or reorganize the practice to serve the niche most effectively. This may require the appointment or addition of a partner who will coordinate activities, monitor trends, and manage the services to meet the expectations of clients and prospective clients. The designated partner should also be responsible for providing any staff training in marketing and utilizing existing engagements to identify additional client needs.

The professions are in a new era that is characterized by rapid and radical changes. The application of strategic management to client-centered marketing will carry professionals through this era and ensure survival and prosperity.

APPENDIX D

Sample Strategic Plan

STRATEGIC PLAN FOR DICK CONNOR, CMC

I. Our Mission

We are a *consulting* firm offering a *broad range of marketing services* and products to clients in the *accounting, consulting,* and public relations *professions*.

Our driving force is *services* and products *offered*.

Our competitive advantage in our marketing is *our reputation within the infrastructures of our targeted profession/markets*.

Our current personal technology is *leading edge* in services and *competitive* in word processing technology for our products.

II. Our Vision

A. Our primary thrust is seeking new clients for our current products in our current targeted professions.

Within our primary thrust, we seek a *broader penetration of current client groups and markets with our current products*.

We seek to *enhance services* and products *based on our core capability* developed from targeted new assignments.

B. Our Desired Future Profile

1. New Clients

We seek new clients who have needs within the scope of our services and products and the following desirable characteristics:

- They are clones of our current best clients—both individual firms and associations.
- They seek, recognize, and will pay for the distinctive values we provide.
- They are within our key targeted profession/markets.
- They provide experiences that can be codified and marketed.

We will not accept new clients that:

- Unduly drain our energies.
- Provide us with undue risk and vulnerability.
- Fall beyond our scope!

2. Geographical Focus

We prefer the following ZIPs and geographic areas for our new business activities:

- Services: Deeper penetration of the Greater Washington, D.C., market area
- Products: North America

3. New Service Development

We will only invest in the development of new services that:

- Provide us with the opportunity to leverage our out-of-office engagement hours by developing products for sale.
- Are interesting to develop, promote, and provide.
- Break even from the start.
- Are extensions of our current best-received services.

4. Positioning—How Do We Want to be Known? By Whom?

We want to be known as a firm that provides practical solutions to the current marketing and management problems faced by the busy professional.

5. Competitive Advantage in the Market

Our competitive advantage *is and will be* our willingness and ability to convert concepts into practical actions and marketing tools and to convey our capabilities in exciting and empowering ways.

6. Marketing Priorities
   a. Developing new client relationships   <u>50%</u>
   b. Deeper penetration of current/previous
      clients with current services   <u>30%</u>
   c. Provision of new services to current clients   <u>10%</u>
   d. Edging into related new client groups   <u>0%</u>
   e. Improving our visibility and positioning in
      current targeted industry ZIPs   <u>10%</u>
                                                           100%

Index

About the Authors

Dick Connor is a certified management consultant serving providers of professional services in marketing and selling their services. For information about his services, you can contact him directly:

Dick Connor, CMC
6711 Bracken Court
Springfield, VA 22152
(703) 569–9139 Office
(703) 569–2566 Fax

Jeff Davidson is a certified management consultant and popular speaker, offering programs on marketing, time management, and personal achievement. For information on his keynote presentations and lectures, call or write to him:

Jeffrey P. Davidson, CMC
3713 S. George Mason Dr. #1216W
Falls Church, VA 22041
(703) 931–1984
(800) 735–1994